THE
PLUME
ANTHOLOGY OF
POETRY
3

edited by Daniel Lawless

MadHat P

ASHEVILLE, NORTI

D1070342

MadHat Press
MadHat Incorporated
PO Box 8364, Asheville, NC 28814

The material in this anthology is selected from
PlumePoetry.com
by Editor Daniel Lawless
with the assistance of Production Managers
Jonathan Penton & FJ Bergmann

ISBN 978-1-941196-16-8 (paperback)

Cover art by Allen Forrest
Dana, oil on canvas panel, 20"x16", 2010

Book and cover design by MadHat Press

PlumePoetry.com
MadHat-Press.com

to reading, which saved me

"*Plume's* apparent lack of a narrow editorial policy (except a fondness for interesting poems) makes for lots of strange bedfellows, but what was the last time that was a bad idea?"
~ *Billy Collins*

"Of all the things that might claim one's attention, and they are in the multitudes! *Plume* is well worth making time for since it isn't just another magazine. Its difference? Wonderful work, on the edge, room for play and dash, new forms, a great discerning editor in Danny Lawless!"
~ *Tess Gallagher*

"*Plume* is one of the most exciting, eclectic gatherings of writers on the web. Editor Daniel Lawless has a knack for putting together voices that create surprising neighborhoods of words, related in complex ways that only gradually reveal themselves. It's one of very few webzines that I always read."
~ *Chase Twichell*

"*Plume* is rapidly becoming one of the best places in America to read poetry, online and in print, thanks to the untiring efforts of Danny Lawless. It's where to find dazzling work by new and established writers, and, thanks to the new technology, it is available instantly to readers by the millions. *Plume* proves once more that poetry is essential to our lives, and that 'Men die every day for want of what is found in it.'"
~ *Grace Schulman*

"*Plume* continues to publish amazing poets in beautiful formats—both online and in-print. The magazine has an exciting vision, embracing a broad gamut of poetries, including collaborations. The work has a consistently intriguing quality about the joys and unsettling aspects of being alive."
~ *Denise Duhamel*

"*Plume* is a new force in the poetry world, bringing together, in its online zine and in this anthology, a unique, eclectic and impressive group of poets."
- *Rae Armantrout*

"I've never seen a literary magazine become so important so quickly. I have no idea how Daniel Lawless does it, but I dare anyone to find another journal that contains 1) the high quality of the individual poems, 2) the wide range of voices and styles, and 3) the large number of leading voices in contemporary American poetry. I would love to see all these poets in the same room, but I'll take them here, all in the same book."
- *Jim Daniels*

"I usually hate to read poems on the computer but *Plume* has changed my mind. It is attractive, well-edited, and possesses the compelling virtue of being concise—not too many poems, not too few. Since I always end up wanting to print out one or two, I'm grateful for Danny Lawless's equally exciting, good-looking, and well-chosen, *Plume* anthologies."
- *Lawrence Raab*

"*Plume* is a gathering place where strangers become old friends. Each issue is a celebration of images and words that touch the heart and bind us together as community."
- *Lawrence Matsuda*

"The first word I remember using to describe Danny Lawless's online *Plume* was the word elegant. And now I discover that the word derives from a Latin verb for *to select*. *Plume* endeavors to select and showcase— yes, elegantly—the best poems of the twenty-first century. *Plume* not only encourages, it honors poetry."
- *Ron Smith*

"*Plume* is a gem—in the rare-and-wondrous-find sense. Each issue is a hand-plucked, precisely curated composition, tended with great care, full of mystery, and delivering batches of the freshest, most provocative, and necessary writing around. Danny Lawless's vision is exquisite."
- Lia Purpura

"Though I've been known to shy away from online publications, I'm an avid reader of *Plume*, a beautifully designed monthly periodical featuring an international selection of works by some of today's best poets. Hard to beat that."
- William Trowbridge

"Plume (Noun): An anthology or journal of fine writing edited with passion and immaculate attention to detail.
"Plume (Verb): To erupt with energy, enthusiasm and poetic spirit. To dazzle.
"Derivative of Plume: Plumelike (Adjective): As fine as down and as lively as peacock feathers.
"Origins of *Plume*: American, but with an internationalist bent, some time during the 2000s."
- John Kinsella

Daniel Lawless has a gift for publishing poets who not only represent the breadth and depth at which the art is practiced today, but who together make—how to say it?—a feisty crowd, their proximity in the pages of *Plume* creating all sorts of surprising angles of vision. There's nothing rote in Daniel's editorial choices, nothing of what Emerson called "a foolish consistency." His assemblages of poems, images, and editorial musings have a hand-crafted, one-of-a-kind feel. That's why there's ever cause for celebration when another *Plume*, whether online or in print, makes its way into the world.
- Clare Rossini

"*Plume* magazine is an anomaly of taste: any literary dwelling that can shelter under one roof a family of poets as distantly related as Rae Armantrout, James Richardson, Kim Addonizio, Jorie Graham, Linda Pastan, G.C. Waldrep, Grace Schulman, Carl Phillips, Sharon Olds, Billy Collins, and more, must be both capacious and *odd*. What in the world unites these writers, one thinks? And then one reads an issue of *Plume* with the dawning recognition what they have in common is Danny Lawless, the founder and editor of this superb new journal. Lawless has the audacity to choose the poets he loves, and believes are writing *good* poetry, no matter on what wildly disparate branch of the family tree he finds them. And then he gets these poets to send him poems. *Plume* establishes its place on the literary scene somewhere above fashion, apart from all questions of Hipster vs. ... whatever. The work within its pages has the unpredictable, idiosyncratic strength of things that haunt, and may endure."
- *Jeffrey Skinner*

"Always astonishing and diverse in content, *Plume* is one of our most elite and essential online journals and a roving museum of contemporary poetry curated by Daniel Lawless. 'Glancing blow' after glancing blow, it makes me hungry, ad infinitum, for the strange and beautiful—and the annual anthology is a sumptuous feast of enduring American poetry."
- *Mark Irwin*

"Like a bird landing in the absent shadow of a bird,
Plume has gorgeously and unabashedly
taken up residence inside an inner vane, an ache
in contemporary poetry, and sunk its hooklets in.
Now many of us cannot exist without it,
so drab and songless does a world without *Plume* seem to seem...."
- *Robin Behn*

"Like *Antaeus* and *Ironwood*, two of the greatest American poetry magazines of the past fifty years, *Plume* is eclectic in the most purposeful and pleasurable of ways. In a very short amount of time, Danny Lawless has made it a 'must-read' like no other. *Plume* is one of my favorite sources for new poetry—online or in print. Thoughtful, entertaining, capacious, with no use for aesthetic axe-grinding, its highly-enriched oxygen will add energy to your life!"
~ *David Rivard*

"Among the new magazines of recent years in print and on-line formats, one—*PLUME*—stands above all the rest and offers us both venues. What a delight it is to read the work of newcomers beside the poems of poets I've followed for years! The eclecticism of the editor's taste never ceases to amaze me. I just used the print anthology in my Advanced Poetry Writing Workshop at Tulane and the students echoed my enthusiasm.
~ *Peter Cooley*

THE PLUME ANTHOLOGY OF POETRY is a wild and lovely gathering of poems and poets. Lawless has pulled together a time and place in a selection of some of the most interesting work being done.
~ *Laura Kasischke*

Elegant *Plume* appeared with the flourish of a cyberquill pen in 2011 and quickly became the place where superlative poets showcase their brightest work. Editor Danny Lawless displays his adoration for electric, emotional and, dare I say, meaningful poetry—and for poets themselves—with all the vigor of a steward of this art. Once a year the revered, sparky, sagacious *Plume* comes into print, subtly changing our cultural foundations. Hold it, read it, and applaud!
~ *Molly Peacock*

Reading *Plume* is like having a conversation with your best friend, your best self, and all the people who love the world in its beauty and craziness.
~ *Barbara Hamby*

PREFACE
Terese Svoboda

Plume number three makes a trinity, a definitive solid three-legged stand on the contemporary. We don't have William Carlos Williams putting one over with his wheelbarrow, Hart Crane running off another six pages of his endless Bridge, Marianne Moore obfusticating, or Lola Ridge railing against executions—that's so a hundred years old, so yesterday. What *Plume* has plucked from its manicured 2014 electronic presence and solicitations are new classics like Rae Armantrout with a prickly pear in "Design Elements," "Fuck You" from Dzvinia Orlowsky, Michael Collier's weird "Funky Stuff," Steven Kramer citing a stomacher in "The Great Chain of Being," the haunting yet forgotten face in "The Face" by Laura Kasischke, a so-polite Bangladeshi in Alicia Ostriker's poem "Bangladesh," Molly Peacock's very moving "How to Say Thank You in French," Sally Ball's line "the lyric loves a thought inside a frame" from the exquisite "Some Verses," Marc Vincenz's vertiginous "mystery meat" in "After the Invention of Polystyrene a Ligurian Goat Crosses the Equator," Jane Springer's shapely "Wrought"—I go on and on. There's much more, and very close to VIDA equality. Is there a theme? Some days you don't want an anthology of baseball poems or eat-with-a-spoon poems on desserts, you want poems that leap at you, surprising you one at a time. The logic between these poems opens into metaphorical possibility, making the whole anthology enterprise a single poem of many voices.

A plume of poetry as I see it, that rises up to waft in the shared air of literature, the exotic bird just flown. Thank you Daniel Lawless who solicits with such acuity, who winnows the inbox, who makes real from *Plume* online what the web only promises: the felt presence, the weight of words on paper, the possibility of frisson between postings, between poems. Scrolling down is never facing the page, and we want to face the page, one to another; we want this plumed cacophony to burst from the bushes alarmed, to startle us.

INTRODUCTION

However humble, every artistic endeavor of any notoriety, or history, if we can use that word for such a short-lived project such as *Plume*, inescapably has its creation myth. And having in previous introductions elaborated, *ad nauseam*, I'm sure, on our "mission" as I saw it, it occurs to me now to offer instead just such an archeology, a few notes on origins of the book you now hold in your hands.

In the summer of 1978, I took a trip out to San Francisco with a rich girl; we'd drive into the city from her family's home in Palo Alto to visit her hyper-cool slightly older sculptor/poet/musician/ activist/vegan/ actor-model brother, who introduced us to all that that mash-up implies. About which I could go on for pages, but for the purposes of this *aide-mémoire* will confine myself to the third in that series of occupations/personae—specifically the punk scene, in which he already was deeply enmeshed—as represented in my memory at least by the dives and holes-in-the-wall to which he escorted us almost nightly, where we saw the Nuns, the Offs, Agent Orange, Negative Trend, Dead Kennedys and other soon-to-be luminaries, each with its own vomitory charms and nascent, planetesimal mosh pits.

Eye and ear-opening to be sure, for a rube-ish quasi-autodidact from Louisville, Kentucky, where slack-jawed cover bands and straw-chewing bluegrass ruled the day. But it was a subset of this experience that was to prove pivotal in my own artistic life, such as it was: the concert posters that these bands produced and affixed to seemingly every available surface in the city. The style: a cliché now, of course, long ago reduced to frame-available Etsy decrepitude, consigned to the dustbin of nostalgia or worse irony. Nevertheless: there it was, an art *in the world*, literally free, toying *in situ* with its victims and all but asking for defacement, itself, or spurious acquisition: available for the taking by any passerby with a nail file or fingertips callused and patient enough to peel paper intact from concrete.

And so when I returned home, what else was for it but to replicate that epiphanic experience, as far as I could? As fortune would have it, as I say, punk had not yet staggered into my hometown, so there still was a certain ... space in which I might maneuver. Never the musical type (though that hardly would have mattered and may have been in fact a *prima facie* disqualifier) or of sufficient social aptitude or ambition to make the necessary arrangements to establish a band, I found myself drawn to the idea of those posters. Equally unburdened, too, of any shred of talent for visual representation, in retrospect it's no wonder I turned my attentions to the fertile gardens of poetry, which I had tended for some time by then (failing, naturally, to coax any of my efforts into the bloom of publication) and which I read obsessively.

My first exhibition was of a self-penned embarrassingly surrealist-indebted poem called, I believe, "Is it you?" ("... whose glove I find on the dark stairs/pointing out the very moment I see in my dreams," etc.) and involved a staple gun and one hundred legal-sized copies provided courtesy of the University of Louisville English Department Xerox machine. My publisher, the Louisville Gas and Electric Company, which kindly offered as pages their telephone poles—in those days all but virginal, save for the odd "Lost Dog" advertisement or apartment-to-let notice with its pocket comb of contact numbers from which one or two might have been extracted like missing teeth. Signed with a hand-carved rubber stamp of a skeletal bird cribbed from a plate in some tome or another, as I wished to remain anonymous, fearing the derision all but certain to follow if my authorship become known. Distributed late one fall evening—giddily —by myself and that girlfriend, a poetry lover and a poet too in a few more years.
     What did I—we—expect? Nothing, really. Which was approximately what we received, at first. For days after that initial outing I would patrol our route as a trapper his lines, looking for signs of struggle—which I did discover, usually in crude amendments and inventively profane commentary. But success? Only occasional—evinced unlike the trapper's not by the presence of his quarry but its

absence. And even that more notional than verified—surely in large part a matter of a property-owner's annoyance, or reflexive vandalism. Yet, once in a while, I would be pleasantly surprised to enter a friend's apartment or pass some forlorn storefront or club to discover my poem magnetized to a refrigerator door or taped to a window. An occurrence, however sporadic, that never failed to delight me, and sufficient in every way to keep the enterprise afloat.

Thus it went, to coin a phrase. When my own poetical inventory was exhausted, I turned to the ready supply of works I had come across in my reading: Trakl's "Winter Evening," Paz's "Motion," passages from Cendrars' "Transsiberian Prose ...," Vallejo's "A man Passes by ...," Char's "The Absent One," poems from Transtromer, Levine, and Martison and Bly's *Silence in the Snowy Fields*, Russel Edson, Merton, St. John of the Cross, and Michaux, parts of *Ubu*, and Barthes' *Mythologies*, Mishima, and Robbe-Grillet—all made appearances. Over the course of perhaps a year I papered Bardstown Road and Frankfort Avenue, the twin drags of what passed for the city's post-hippie bohemia, with dozens of poems.

And then, inevitably and overnight, as it must have seemed in every American town of any size from Greenville to Corvalis, punk was everywhere, first incarnated in Louisville by No Fun, a group hailing from—where else?—the local art school. Followed quickly by a slew of other iterations—Poor Girls, The Dickbrains, The Endtables— all with their own posters *à la mode*, which in short order appeared on those upright billboards, overlapping my beloved Tzara one day, replacing Reverdy the next.

I was done.

Now: fast-forward thirty-five years, to find your author, after innumerable false starts and hiatuses intentional and otherwise, ensconced in a professorial position, teaching Creative Writing in a small college while continuing his "real" if unrecompensed employment: writing poetry, and reading—always reading. A student in the back row scrolling porn—but no, as I discovered when I wandered over to impart an admonishing word. Instead, *Pank*. A literary 'zine, whose "mission" he, the student, wished me to know and which I read for myself: "To the end of the road, up country, a far shore, to the edges of things, to a place of amalgamation and unplumbed depths, a place inhabited by contradiction, quirk and startling anomaly, where the known is made and unmade, and where unimagined futures are born."

Beautiful, yes?

And there it was. 1977 become 2011. To say my mind raced, an understatement. For what was this but an electronic redux of those long-ago days of poem-hanging, the editor, Matt Bartley Seigel, as I would learn, introducing or reintroducing readers to those poets and poems he clearly loved, as I had in those long-ago days? A quick meeting in my office was arranged then and there, to further my education, visiting half a dozen other such sites which had somehow eluded me, fogey that I was and am, and the revelation that my erstwhile guide— Jason Cook, *Plume*'s now-Managing Editor—could put together a website for a minimal fee (though many hours spent in design and layout at Starbucks).

And so, *Plume*. Not anonymous this time; and drawing on an inventory not only of work, however obscure, already published, but *new* poems from *new* poets (and old ones too) I have chanced upon over the intervening years, whose mastery moved me as those early poems' had. Whose authors—astonishingly, given their capital-*r* Reputations, many of them—responded with startling alacrity and goodwill to my hastily penned requests for work, *gratis*, needless to say—why, I'll never know; or slipped over the transom via Submittable. (And have continued to do so, for nearly four years.) Yet, these are trivial distinctions, I think. In the end, and in spirit, this book—our third annual anthology(!)— remains very much a successor to those early guerrilla poetry forays —how quaint that phrase even as I write it, in this age of slams and "poetry parking tickets"—its tidy pages suffused in my mind with the night air and a certain perfume my accomplice wore, as we made our way along those deserted streets, in love perhaps, with each other and with the fantastical notion that poetry could change and charge others as it had us.

Daniel Lawless
Editor, *Plume*
23 January 2015

CONTENTS

NEIGHBOR
~ translated by Alex Cigale

The old asthmatic who had lost his mind last year
is sitting on the balcony. Like a flower he
knows only what directly touches him. A howl
brings only his throat to life, and the blood, like an ambush,
accosts the pupils. Who inhabits him now? What
sly intelligence forces the nagging cough out of him
onto the bloodless street? His face grimaces
into a desiccated compacting clump that will any moment now
disappear transposing into a different reality. What makes him cry
    out—whose heel
tramples with increasing intensity his soul?
Whose will extracts him out of the ancient well
and flings him anew to the bottom of the vertical tunnel? His hands
converge but not in a gesture of embrace,
the joints of the fingers moaning. When he feels better,
he is
a bird in a nest.

СОСЕД
~ original by Shamshad Abdullaev

Старик-астматик, сошедший с ума в прошлом году,
сидит на балконе. Он, словно цветок,
знает лишь то, что к нему прикасается. Вопль—
оживает одно только горло, и кровь, как засада,
встречает зрачки. Кто в нём теперь? Какой
хитрый разум выталкивает из него злой кашель
на бескровную улицу? Его лицо сжимается
в сухой комок всё ýже, вот-вот исчезнет,
перейдёт в другую реальность. Отчего он кричит—чья ступня
давит с нарастающей силой на его
душу? Чья воля извлекает его из древнего колодца
и вновь бросает на дно вертикального туннеля? Его руки
сходятся, но не в знаке объятья,
стонут суставы пальцев. Когда ему легче,
он—
птица в гнезде.

THE OUTSKIRTS
~ translated by Alex Cigale

No overriding concern. A woman,
her hair worn down, is washing dishes. Clanging, flaxen eye brows
    furrowed
together, above her head
a Yellow Everlasting. And silence, that cannot be overtaken,
even by force. At
the water pump, a boy has donned a fake beard, like some kind of pygmy
who had accepted the Christian faith. This, not the South
but a humid, golden mischief, and the glutinous segments of dead beetles
are scattered on the ground. A wide alleyway between walls
(where the road is visible,
angled downhill)—an incidental emptiness. A hoopoe
alights on the wooden handrail and the landscape's center shifts toward
the bird: a stirred up,
prophetic, little crown of feathers. From the window
of your small room all this appears a part
of the household mythology (your
favorite phrase). A record revolves. Objects
gag on the music that had at once deciphered
our world. One wants
to fold one's palms together in prayer:
atonement, atonement. A passerby
flings a fleeting glance into the open window, and this is sufficient, so that
one might begin to speak of that which bears no
relevance to momentariliness. Your
Socratic pranks: to listen,
listen and then suddenly cram the entire present landscape
into a single charming phrase. The bird
continues to trouble us
with the inescapable nature of a zoological metaphor.
The outskirts.

ОКРАИНА
~ original by Shamshad Abdullaev

Никакой идеи. Простоволосая
женщина моет посуду. Звон, белые сросшиеся брови, над
    головой
жёлтый бессмертник. И тишина, которую не возьмёшь
даже приступом. У
водопроводного крана мальчик напялил фальшивую бороду,
    словно пигмей,
принявший христианскую веру. Это не Юг,
а душная, золотая проказа, и клейкие сегменты мёртвых жуков
разбросаны по земле. Широкий проход между стен
(где видно дорогу,
идущую под уклон)—залётная пустота. На перильное дерево
садится удод, и центр пейзажа перемещается к птице:
    разбуженный,
вещий хохолок. Из окна
твоей комнатёнки всё это выглядит частью
домашней мифологии (твоё
любимое словечко). Вращается пластинка; предметы
давятся музыкой, вычитающей сразу
наш мир. Хочется
в молитвенной клятве ладони сложить:
смилуйся, смилуйся. Прохожий
бросает мимолётный взгляд в окно, и этого достаточно, чтобы
заговорить о том, что не имеет
отношения к мимолётности. Твои
сократовские выходки: слушать,
слушать и внезапно втиснуть весь тутошний ландшафт
в одну очаровательную фразу. Птица
продолжает морочить нас
навязчивостью зооморфной метафоры.
Окраина.

No Reason
~ Kim Addonizio

I could die at any moment,
so why not drink until I achieve
a state of incoherent idiocy
is a question that has been asked before,
but never satisfactorily answered.
Live the questions, Rilke counseled the young poet
who promptly disappeared into obscurity,
proving that literary advice is useless,
like explaining to your goldfish
how to use the remote.
Nevertheless, remember that many adverbs
are on drugs and trying to pick your pocket.
Because life is briefer than a squirrel orgasm
I would like to go to Lisbon
and get morbidly drunk in Portuguese
beneath the statue of Pessoa
that wears a book for a face.
Whether we are swan flutes and lyre-shaped goblets
or random collections of beach glass
is another question that puzzles many.
Did I mention I could die at any moment?
Why not rape that girl and her mother
asks the soldier, after seeing his buddy
blasted open like a piñata.
Then again, asks nurse Whitman,
why not hold everyone's hand
and enjoy the fresh towels?
Sometimes a car lets you into its lane,
sometimes you get a homemade Valentine
instead of a jury summons.

Stevens said death is the mother,
but what kind of mother is she?
Take a look at her children
and tell me what you see.

LANDSCAPE IN A LANDSCAPE
~ Kelli Russell Agodon

I could spend every Friday night drinking Frank O'Hara and reading
red wine, a New York hangover not happening
in New York, but here by the sea where you are
gorgeous and I am late for an outside dinner
near the camellia.

By the time I arrive, the women are bewitched
by blossoms slipped into their cleavage and the men
with flowers tucked behind their ears. Everyone blooms,
everyone comments on the dapper fresh cut grass.

It's almost an old romance with blue sky
endings, all those French pastry clouds that fill me, enough,
so I want to fall onto a blanket and put my hands on anyone
who gives me a whisper, a little glimmer proving this
is not a memory.

Even now, the flame from the ripped page I carry
in my dress pocket warms my perfume and while you think
I mistake you for a stranger, what can I say?

After all these years, I will always recognize you
and what blooms near your receding hairline. In your eyes,
I see you grieving for our past, just as I do, and the moon rises,
and someone collects our plates, and someone pours more wine,
and somehow we end up together again.

INFIRMARY
~ Sandra Alcosser

Instead of a sulfuric chemistry
Test mimeographed on purple sheets

From a spirit duplicating machine—

We bedded down beneath vaulted ceilings—
Palladian glass arching inside Andover Cream—
And believed it possible to sail white sheets
Out the window and through the stately trees
With nothing more to tether us than the squeak
Of Nursey's gum shoes
As she trayed yet another glass of juice

Years later it will all return—how I hid
In sickness, how it began a first delicious
Recess from class and loud laughter and keeping
Up—first flight to capture the hot fever of being

BRIGHT PASSAGE
~ Meena Alexander

I.

Grandmother's sari, freckles of gold poured into silk,
Koil's cry, scrap of khadi grandfather spun,
I pluck all this from my suitcase, its buckles dented, zipper torn.
Also pictures pressed into an album:
Parents by a rosebush,
Ancestors startled in sepia, eyes wide open,
Why have you brought us here?

II.

Mist soars on the river, my door splits free of its hinges:
My children's children, and those I will never see,
Generations swarm in me,
Born to this North American soil, dreamers in a new world.
I must pass through that rocking doorway,
Figure out words, clean minted, untranslatable—
Already in the trees finches are warbling, calling my name.

NOTE:
This poem was specially composed for the exhibit Beyond Bollywood: Indian
Americans Shape the Nation, Smithsonian, Washington DC, 2014–2015. The first
stanza of the poem appears on the wall of the exhibit on the left, just as you enter,
above a trunk filled with various articles a migrant might have brought with her.

THE DRESS-MAKER OF GALILEE
~ Kazim Ali

He wears himself down and becomes wild uncertain
Laps the frayed thread-end
With his clumsy tongue

He wants to know as well what the body
and its covering will teach him about
genders of flesh

The Druze have a secret book
Some know what's in it, some don't
But no one minds

His voice falls into pieces when he claims
For himself the spaces
Of flowers or silk

At the silver thread of the border between
what was and what wasn't some Druze know
We are all about to switch genders

With eyes of smoke and his tailor's needle
In the globe of barbarous heat
He stakes his claim in stitches

He never learned how to behave
Only to stitch every piece
And spike heaven sense

NATURE
~ Ralph Angel

Looking through trees strangely into nature.

A window, an air-conditioner, a wall covered with ivy.

The book on your lap. Your head tilted back.

Like handling cups or pennies, a shovel, a stone.

Like where an arm is found, or where the tangled limbs go.

A bookshop, a fruitstand. You wake up and there you are, and there
you are.

"Do we have any cookies, or something nice?"

Toward the east outstretches the shadow. On the left a plywood lake.

Gods and horses playing in the fountain. A conch shell. A robe.

The swallows, the sandstorms, a pink fire in the clouds.

And the generator, the chain and the pulley. Unheard-of laughter and
prayer.

The long exhalation. Of baskets and flutes.

Of bracken. Of reed. Of cypress and olive, pelvis and spine.

Three shoes on a doorstep. Of human unfinished.

The spirit in time.

DESIGN ELEMENTS
~ Rae Armantrout

Green faces
of the prickly pear

like oval hand mirrors
set at angles

(and, of course,
spotted with thorns).

Each face has a large
topknot—

a bud.

    *

A few titular
poles or pikes,

some with frou-frou
fronds on top

catching late sun.

    *

I like it
when the clouds

are retro—

puffs and dashes
of Morse Code.

God's faux messages,
all in fun.

FLOOD
~ David Baker

       Immensity of song—to be so small
that throat—
       that singer   wren on a red
tree—
       amid the wicks of wet fruit.
And a light comes up
       in and out of the houses
I hung there.
       In and out,
of climbing hydrangea,

       each house-hole *trumpeting*
like loud flowers
       the size of a quarter—
all week, flitting
       through hanging ferns, cocked tail,
blunt chest. What big
       song.
And the little birds,
       brown as buns,
in and around the trees—

       You want to keep a lot
of water out
       what?—is what he said.
Yes of course. All
       I could think was wings,
but that's not
       true. But partly
also this, the end of it, what we'd been,

       rain in
the night not rain but sheets,

       wild, torrents
claiming every dry thing until
       buckled there the very under-
pinning of the house. Yes
       faster than the pumps.
Easy, he said, block
       auger—*weep-holes* is what he said—
backhoe pickaxe you want to keep a lot of water
       out *bright song* let
a little in—

SOME VERSES
~ Sally Ball

[on Hiroshi Senju's *Day Falls / Night Falls* and *Cliff*]

Light vs. Dark

    Lyric vs. Discursive

        Language vs. Disco!

        Lark vs. Dodo—

        There it is:
        song and extinction.
        Bits and zeros
        lay down each warbled track.

Like to the lark at break of day

(First poem I ever had by heart,
thirty years now of my swimming in its DNA,
it swimming in mine—)

From sullen earth sings hymns at heaven's gate

For the record, the lyric isn't just compression,
like those running tights, the lyric
loves a thought inside a frame. Arrival,
containment. A canvas stretched so taut
it pushes light away.

Arising

Look at Senju's two paintings:

vast black-and-whites, one the daunting mountain
with its shadow-copse, a hiking story, the Sublime;
the other an X-ray of maybe what a thought looks like,
what distraction looks like spilling its white smoke,
its wet white smoke in rivulets. Smoke falls, it wafts,
it blocks our easy looking toward the dark. We shuffle
up identities in order to stay alive here, the mind's keen
eye goes in, toward the faraway black dark, but never
passes through the veil. What we want, and how we're
separate from that, which makes it possible to want
at all, it all. The veil of what else, what else—
                                                    "I see you."
That's what this painting says to whoever looks. Not mirror, not
yet: it just sees me. Or you. And lets us know, *Haply*

I think on thee

The mountain is discursive: it's even a story, each crag
qualifies some detail, adds plot or texture, admits
or claims a point-of-view. The X-ray of attention,
that's the lyric utterance, abstract, seducing by usurpment
of my mind (my mind is mine, then Senju's, then mine, then his—)
and then my state,   for thy sweet love,   such wealth brings

But *we* don't scorn to change our state with kings
                    —not for love and not for money—

in fact we like to disappear, and to "identify."
And art incites such eagerness to relinquish
self,
        goodbye, goodbye, hello, hello

I'm in disgrace with fortune.

And men's eyes.

I all alone beweep—

And now you see it too. The lyric makes it ours together, fuses us.
Look: the dark, anyone can say it's there; anyone can point. What
    frightens

us is all that mediation. All that filtered light.

The song of my pending extinction permits my staying alive.

Stayin' alive.

Ah ah ah ah—

AUBADE
~ translated by David Colmer

for Piet Piryns

We talk until we see the morning double.
The bar is spinning from the cigarettes.
A dishcloth on the tap is wrung and sleepy.
'If I knew who I was, I wouldn't be me.'

We make our way with straight backs to the toilet.
Ah, l'orgasme du pauvre … The river runs dry.
The front door yawns about the morning paper.
Another man is aping death.

Ah, friendship's demented reign of terror!
Few dare to raise their voice against the heavens,
many will see the sparrow fall and not reach out their arms
(although the barmaid with the dimples has her charms).
We'll take our knives to the wind that blows her any harm!

And now we've nothing else to do, let's raise a hollow glass to the
        mothers
we bury deeper and deeper in the iron anecdotes of childhood,
remembering with a smile that wasted longing for a South
beneath the silver clouds, iconostasis of these steaming lands …
And to our fathers, murdered so much more than necessary!

'I've written a book, but haven't read it.'
'No one told us who we were.'
We scrape our hearts out till they're empty.
We mumble like Jews.

The day is white as dough.
I stare with stinging eyes
at the gods' gold watch,
hung between the fraying clouds:

the time is three thousand years in Europe.

AUBADE
~ original by Benno Bernard

Voor Piet Piryns

We praten tot we blauw zien van de ochtend.
De kroeg is draaierig van de sigaretten.
Een vaatdoek hangt over de tapkraan te slapen.
'Als ik wist wie ik was, was ik een ander.'
We wankelen kaarsrecht naar de toiletten.
Ah, l'orgasme du pauvre ... Het water zwijgt.
De voordeur staat te geeuwen van de krant.
Een derde man ligt de dood na te apen.

O, het zachtzinnige schrikbewind van de vriendschap!
Weinigen durven te spreken tegen de hemel,
velen zullen de mus wel zien vallen en haar niet vangen
(maar mogelijk de barmeid met de kuiltjes in haar wangen).
Wij zetten het mes in de wind die haar optilt!

En nu we toch niets doen, drinken we holle glazen
          op onze moeders,
die we dieper en dieper begraven in de ijzeren anekdote
          van onze jeugd,
en herinneren ons glimlachend dat ijdele verlangen
          naar een zuiden
onder de zilveren wolken, van deze dampende landen
          de iconostase ...
En op onze vaders, zoveel vermoorder dan hoefde!

'Ik heb een boek geschreven, maar het niet gelezen.'
'Niemand heeft ons verteld wie wij waren.'

We schrapen de rest van ons hart leeg.
We murmureren als joden.

De dag is wit als deeg.
Ik kijk met mijn bijtende ogen
op het grote horloge van de goden,
dat tussen gerafelde wolken hangt:

het is drieduizend jaar in Europa.

DOUBLE EXPOSURE WITH SPIRIT PHOTOGRAPHS & SUMMER JOB

~ Ciaran Berry

In the pocket of my porter's uniform, I kept it like an amulet, a lucky charm—
that glass bauble cut to a fake diamond from the chandelier's suspended midair
shower. Trinket. Gewgaw. Ersatz harbinger. I turn it over once more in my palm,

finger and thumb it until it breaks the skin. I climb the wobbly stepladder again
with my Windowlene, my bucket of used towels—details that might help frame me
in that place, that time, which is Eastbourne, which is the tail end of a century,

a striped deckchair and a melted ice cream cone, our maitre d', who came
from Krakow or Poznan, trying his tongue around "another day, another dollar"
as we wash our hands before the same crooked mirror on the ground floor

of The Mansion. All this week, I've been trying to make sense of *Leviathan*,
Hobbes's lush and rambunctious sentences, his conception of how memory
makes, of each of us, a girl sweeping a hotel room in search of a lost earring,

a lost pearl; how memory makes, of each of us, a springer spaniel ranging
the field until it finds the scent. All this week, I've been staring at images
in which, some sleight of hand, trick of the lens, the dead rest a wet palm

23

on the shoulder of the living, all slicked back hair and hats and Sunday best,
the photograph a means by which they might let us know they continue to exist.
And so, the lost wife, who shows up behind her bereft husband. And so, the son,

much missed, come back from the front on Armistice without a scratch. Like
this, the past creeps up on the present. Light of a sudden where no light had been,
a face rising from silver salts and gelatin to cleave the air above the cenotaph.

A secretary conjuring out of your grief, the clippings from a magazine, the cut
and paste figure of a lost love. Call it the catch and drag of pure fancy, a man
running over the alphabet in search of an apt rhyme: the shutters of the eye

close and open on the carcasses that sway in the cold room, on the kitchen
where my friend, the pearl diver, dipped through soapsuds for knives and forks
and spoons, while the breakfast chef, an ex-merchant seaman, divided us

Paddy from Taff and Pole from Czech. Once more, I rise and fall between floors
with the equine features of the night porter who could hear the dead whisper
and bitch in the elevator shaft, who could see them wander the early morning

corridors looking for something lost, something mislaid. Once more, I bear,
down or up the backstairs, a plate of toast, touched or untouched, a knob of butter,
for our most famous guest, a mid-ranked tennis player who's lost once more.

I can hear the ball as it snags in the net cord, its pock against the racket's mesh
of strings, the umpire saying "Sir, please sit down so play can resume." I can taste
salt spray, warm English rain, a whole world opening at the prompt of my tongue

with something like the same backward longing that might raise the dead, settle
them in the frame, double-exposed. Think Hobbes's idea of the centaur as a man's
body superimposed, by memory, over the body of a horse, of how the past is

a circle we can't square. Think of the mothball and blue rinse old dears laying
down, one over the other, their chested cards in the ballroom's crushed splendor,
a nighttime game of gin. The eight, nine, ten of hearts. The jack, queen, king.

THE BIRD TRAP
~ Linda Bierds

after the painting by Pieter Brueghel the Younger

But for clusters of red clothing, the painting
is monochrome, snow and river
in that ivory-going-to-gray a winter evening offers.
And under the evening, under
the sky and smoky horizon, traversing
the painting's lower half, deep snow and the frozen river
exactly divide the scene:
two dozen birds near a riverfront yard, six of them flying;
two dozen people on the ice, six with arms extended.
And under their laughter and guttural chirrups
lies nothing but the scrape of skates
and the dull chatter of curling stones
as they slip, like great rounds of granite bread,
toward some gradually vanishing target
etched on the scored ice.
                    *   *

Movements Alan Turing would love, had he seen the painting.
The balancing figures, of course, and the curler,
bent to a stone, putting a little English on it.
But also the target, invisibly sinking away—
rings, inner rings, and a center button—becoming
at last just a pattern in the mind.
                    *   *

It is 1952. The charge: gross indecency. The parlor:
cluttered. On a cheap violin, Turing is playing
"Cockles and Mussels", the music's wordless barrow
scraping past Wills and Rimmer, two seated detectives
who cannot stop mouthing sweet Molly Malone. Why not,

for these minutes, listen, the bugger so welcoming,
so quick to confess, as if two men together…as if
two men complicitly trying
the three condemned exchanges Turing so openly listed,
were free? And isn't it almost legal, he asked,
and who is displaced, the world so shattered
we must speak in codes, in key clicks and ciphers,
rings, inner rings, the bow lifted, his unshaven chin
on the rest, breath in, breath out, fogging
the body, fogging the thin, yellowed,
almost mother-of-pearl varnish, over
and over, alive, alive-o.

     *   *

Two perils: in the lower left foreground
a large, dark hole in the ice; in the lower right
a bird trap—a heavy, wooden door
propped up at one end by a stick.
It makes a little lean-to, a little respite
in the snow, its soft floor sprinkled with seeds,
and its trip-rope, tied to the stick, so pale
in the winter yard that Turing must step closer,
must place his face near the old wood
and stiffened leather hinges
to see the rope arc upward—from the stick, through
the yard, then on through a narrow window
where someone invisibly watches.
Or doesn't. The window so close to the painting's edge
the trap seems harmless, unmanned, a simple
geometric shape, a kind of static pendulum
set to capture the turning world. And did they know,

     *   *

Turing asked, that the proper way
to launch a pendulum's bob
is by thread and candle flame? The bob

tied above its downward arc, the candle
burning through the tie. Foucault—more wine?—
knew this. Did they? No chance for interference then.
No clammy hands or coughs or tics.
No common human veerings.

*   *

The house is almost outside the scene. A slice
of wall and roofline, a slash of bird-blind window.
In the foreground, left and right,
two perils, passive: allegory's lolling greed.

*   *

One takes the utmost care, he said.
Clear path. Near-windless room. Star shape
painted on the floor to illustrate the journey.
Symmetry. Trajectory.
Bright candle. Silk thread.

HEART ATTACK
~ Sally Bliumis-Dunn

Our father left us with his heart—

by then, a pale weak thing we never got

to tend before he died;

it hung in the summer air

like an abandoned nest;

and it is useless

to be sad. Though I am sad—

in the air above the fields

yellow edged wings

an aubergine mourning cloak—

my father would have shown me

how to pinch its thorax, pin it

on the spreading board and wait

as if it would be, somehow

less dead, more enshrined

in my own hands.

Ssh!
~ Stephen Todd Booker

Label me the ungrateful wretch—
I, who've worn a much stupider look
Than ever I've been stamped upon
My over sixteen-damned-thousand
Days and still counting of hearing
Her father's "Daddy is home," as I
Crouched in her closet, and his "How's
My cupcake," then his groan, tasting,
Savoring his daughter's mouth. Ssh!

Put your hand here. Do you feel that?
It's where my heart has sagged ever since.
Some kind of pay dirt, this is, eh,
My soul squished into a corner,
Hemmed in underneath side-by-side
Small skirts and GSA uniforms,
Hammocked in my gutful of Oh?
Later that year, she bore a son,
The spit and image of … you've guessed.

He'd be in his mid-forties now,
And I so hope he honors nothing
Invisible, though is as blessed
As not knowing too much can be.
But what's to be educed from you,
Science, that's pretending to advance
Theories to a child who before
He could spell his name read labels,
Brand names, and colors of crayons

Smacked into his piping? Forgive
Him for failing to compare horrors—
Like, I betcha could maybe spell
Most everykinda grease there is,
Cold creams, and sometimes shortening,
Jellies, jams, and preservatives, huh,
And syrups and honeys?—You must
Turn this page on that little child
Leading you but to a mirror.

BAPTIST WOMEN
~ David Bottoms

My mother loves to talk about her health—in eighty-six years

seven major surgeries, two fractured hips,
five ribs, one ankle, assorted broken fingers and toes.

The church ladies who visit
don't seem to mind. They have their own maladies.

Outside the planet heats up, though it's not yet summer.
Squirrels thunder all afternoon on the roof.

My mother says something about the voice of God
rumbling in her hearing aid.

She also heard it two weeks ago, a wave in the static
of the emergency room—drip, hum, drip, hum.

A Baptist lady unwraps a casserole.

My mother loves to talk about her heart.
The church ladies who visit don't seem to mind.

They have their own maladies, or relatives who have them.
All saints suffer. It's common knowledge.

Nowy Targ
~ Daniel Bourne

Out in the fields, this is not necessarily Poland, despite
the smell of black manure and the white bird before you,
the stork

that may or may not be a messenger
as it follows the farmer,
hoping for a tasty
scared-up frog.

Just another banker in a white shirt,
the stork flaps its wings, settles
on a few words. "O little frog," it says,
"how far to Nowy Targ?"

The frog just gulps, and the farmer

too says nothing, the last man in Galicia
without a tractor, his depressed horse dreaming

of only simple things: a barn in winter.
Grain without the mice.

A field that though he still has to plow it
only goes downhill.

First Day of Retirement—Sitting in My Car at the Beach During a Storm
~ Christopher Buckley

> *Science is a wonderful thing if one does not have to earn one's living at it.*
>
> —Albert Einstein

I find it hard to believe
               there's not some committee meeting
where I am due
        to review the performance objectives
                  of something
as obvious as the clouds …
           it's hard to believe this is me
                  in the rear view
mirror, hair the color of clouds,
             hard equally to believe
                 that
there are shining waters.…

                Just up the tracks from here
I found Tuck Schneider
         half-conscious on the roadside,
cheekbone crushed,
         wheel locked up on his Honda as he crossed
the rails
      50 years ago …
         we had learner's permits
             and motor bikes,
no helmets then, and were free
         to ride aimlessly through our days.
I'd delayed a minute,
        there in the little turn-around,

reaching out

a bit longer for something
limitless,
just beyond the waves....

Invisible, of course,
the incontestable stars,
the shifts and dodging

reconfigurations
of fate—
all that speculation,
now so many

metaphysical smudges,
clouds of breath against the windshield glass....

Nevertheless,
I am still here,
wasting more time with the sky,

the wind taking nothing
lightly.
My blood tastes of salt

and a little rust
where I've absent-mindedly bitten my cheek.

I turned up a hundred
ways to express
my fear of death,

and placed them
amid the dazzling silk trees
and jacarandas,

among the streetlights,
that gauze and yellow glow
from Uncle Codge's

short wave radio
back there in the old country
of childhood

where I recited Latin,

                    mastering the conjugations
of the vainglorious dead
                    where the Hittites came up in Anatolia
with the initial public offering
              for iron,
                    where Juvenal refined satire,
and thus political observation,
              warning too late even then
of bread and circuses....

                  I'm watching the gulls and terns
lift into the pearl-dull sky,
              nonchalant, without a thread
                    of theory
to their names,
          feeling, it would seem, that it's fine
                    to glide about
and look for nothing
            for a time.
              50-some years of guess work
and you'd think I'd have
              an idea about what everything comes to?
There's no shortage
            of imaginative supposition,
                  organized or
otherwise....
       But I'm as flummoxed as the next one,
                despite my
devotion to Albert Einstein—
           first-rate hero
              of the working class,
who quit his boring job
          in the patent office,
              and thought for a living,

and who was never out of work.

Sockless and irreverent,
he was nonetheless determined
to interpret the fine print
and footnotes
of God's thoughts,
possessed as he was
of an empirical faith
in the imagination,
believing
there was something
ultimately there to read....
But he came up short
before the Grand Unified Field,
regretting
finally what they did
with the elegant distillation of light
and matter
he'd managed to decode.
Had he foreseen
the politics,
the fine grind of inhumanity
sewn into the atomic lining
of each
administrator's suit,
he would have quit sooner and turned to playing
his violin alone in the kitchen,
turned to badminton in the back yard
with old cosmologist pals
to whom
he did not have to speak
English
or explain the elliptical transcendence

of a shuttlecock.

On this side,
or some other,
how empty our hands
finally seem to be.
Each evening, a few grey strings
tangle about
the leftovers
of the sea,
the shells and kelp,
such riches as I am left
to busy myself with
before the wind—
the daily indeterminate
sands revealing all
there might be
about intention,
about the body
as a sustainable means
of transport for
a curious or industrious mind.

A last paragraph of dusk pads out
its sleeve-worn *au revoir*,
pavement darkening,
black grease spots,
the ellipses of memory....
Each moment in the universe,
burning away
as if it were nothing,
and we little more
than that for noticing
the relative effects,

the chain link of light,

our impoverished gazing....

Just a few humid layers of air

keep us

from the stars,

from a bright

relapse into dust ...

the incomprehensible everywhere

about us

like clouds,

stalled, then shuffling aimlessly around,

looking

for something to do.

GOAT
~ Michael Burkard

just wanted to tell you that even
if you do the project on the criminologist

whose pet project is the photography
of rare bugs—even if a dahlia bites

the garden's dust for you—
even if you tromp through some

unicorn's hedge on a hedgeless
but murdered afternoon—

even with alas besides
you forsook me a very very long time

ago—so long ago that the past tense
of forsaken doesn't even need apply

MICHAEL BURKARD
~ Michael Burkard

I don't love you enough often enough—Attila Jozsef who began his self portrait
"I really love you, / believe me" may be closer to the attitude I need.

I couldn't even name this without wondering if I am naming myself incorrectly.
Part of me—maybe the missing part—says write your name as Michael Paul Burkard.

By doing so I would include my father and the father part of myself. If this is not
correct—simply off or wrong—it still names another version of myself. A version maybe

too hidden, or mirrored improperly, or incorrectly, or simply not mirrored enough.
My father often called me "Mitch"—I spent many years wondering why—was it his

choice for a name and he had been overruled? My mother didn't seem like the
overruling type. I think of the moon as overruling, the sun as unruly, the world as overturned

by rulers. Rulers of course make me think of the hard-nosed teachers who would have
preferred to strike you with something rather than teach you. But they also settled for and

in the dominant darkness they chose—they sat on the edges of darkening desks—even
in the early morning required light of school the desks which were sat upon by these thugs

had already taken on a darker than normal hue—they settled for threats and chills and
something to take your breath away if they could manage it—they are the ones who had

forgotten their own childhoods—they were no longer a memory including childhood.
Of course as I say this I realize they were probably ruled by hard rulers themselves – more

mean than most probably. My father was not mean. He had been around much mean-
ness but he had early on adopted the survival mode of how to be quiet and non-descript

and even invisible if need be. He need be-d often. I have in my possession a beautiful
picture of my father holding a butterfly net, wearing a cap, and in his other hand he is hold-

ing propped against his chest a small collection of butterflies under glass. He is both
tender and proud. Sadly for me the glass of the collection is reflecting the sun a little too

much—I had the photograph rephotographed but could still not quite make it dark
enough for the butterflies to show more clearly. Or for a little more of his own features to

show slightly. My father has probably saved my world a thousand times and I have not thanked him or thanked him enough. I would love to do something illegal to make you

alive and well another set of years. We could interview those sitting on the edges of their dark desks—maybe like me they need a break from themselves.

AND STORIES
~ translated by John Taylor

from *Ma questo* [But this], *Opere Poetiche*, vol. 2, 1966

And stories, while coming and going
comes and goes. Corpses
sitting on the ground, in dialect
breaking off a violet, a distant violet statue
both lost elsewhere.
While the temples blush
blood-red.

E RACCONTI
~ original by Lorenzo Calogero

E racconti, ma il viavai
va e viene. Sono corpi morti
qua a terra seduti. Si rompono
in dialetto una violetta, una lontana
statua viola perdute insieme
altrove. Ma sono rosso sangue le tempie.

AT A RIGHT ANGLE TO THE VOID
~ translated by John Taylor

from *Come in dittici* [As in diptychs], *Opere Poetiche*, vol. 1, 1962

At a right angle to the void
were footmarks, limits, and hereabouts
the wind, in meadows where things
I cannot recall cannot be heard;
and you know how boring a branch was
and it leads me and divides me
from the air I dislike. I no longer recognize
a veiled presence of being,
a custom of growing and not enough:
if I stop briefly, a whiff
was already too much and all the rest. Winding
and wakeful the tree's vain breathing
also corrupts me in a varied sweetness.
A smoothness that appears in space,
suffering from the void, the disorder, the descent
of the dying age. A breath grew again in the heavy dew.

The implied calls, a breath of air,
a solitude are already listening.

In a cloud like this one,
as far as I know,
your presence has fallen from grace,
like suffering from the vigil
of its flight.

PERPENDICOLARMENTE A VUOTO
~ original by Lorenzo Calogero

Perpendicolarmente a vuoto
tracce erano, limiti, e da questa parte
il vento, in prati ove non si odono
cose di cui non mi ricordo;
e sai quanto noioso un ramo
era e mi guida e dall'aria
mi divide che non amo. Più non riconosco
una larvata presenza di essere,
un'usanza di crescere e non basta:
se mi soffermo un poco un soffio
era già troppo e il resto. Sinuoso
e sveglio un vano respiro d'albero
corrompe me pure in una dolcezza varia.
Una levigatezza che apparve nello spazio
soffre il vuoto, il disordine, il discendere
dell'età morente. Un alito ricrebbe nella guazza.

I sottintesi richiami un respiro d'aria,
una solitudine già odono.

Nella nebbia, per quanto so
ora, come in questa, è partita
la tua presenza dalla grazia
come la sofferenza dalla veglia
del suo volo.

CLOTHES, FLAPPING HATS
~ translated by John Taylor

from *Ma questo* [But this], *Opere Poetiche*, vol. 2, 1966

Clothes, flapping hats
and gloves they're wearing
and the breath of a song
that beats on their brows
and withholds the sad shine
in their eyes; and if the winds
are borderless, the muses alight, look,
on the red roof tiles; and peaks
and fantastic cities stay joyful
now that a vain little girl
pours out the oil from a vain lamp
and lands lost to time
groan in a light dimming them
in a vain chase.

ABITI, SVOLAZZANTI CAPPELLI
~ original by Lorenzo Calogero

Abiti, svolazzanti cappelli
e guanti portano e l'alito
di una canzone che batte in fronte
e il mesto bagliore degli occhi
trattiene; e se i venti
sono senza confine, ecco,
sulle tegole rosse, appaiono
leggere le muse; e cime
e città fantastica stanno con gioia,
ora che olio versa
da una vana lucerna una vana fanciulla
e paesi persi del tempo
in una luce che li smorza gemono
in una vana rincorsa.

THE END OF YOUR SENTENCE
~ Peter Campion

I don't know how
           after such shattering

after the concertina wire and guard towers
recede to glints in the rear view

you patch a life together

      *

but need to tell you:

      *

here where we come from

I have felt this tremble
strike for moments through salt mist

like a falling
        shiver before surrendering to sleep

      *

as all stands chillier but clearer:

      *

releases

to that open element

    the body enters
ignorant of blame

and endings
        as the seals

rising through surf
together with their

flippers and whiskered snouts

and their flared eyes all pupil.

ODE TO A YOUNG MARINER
~ translated by Hélène Cardona

to my brother Manuel
from *El bosque de Birnam* (Consell Insular d'Eivissa, 2007)

The sea is a bride with open arms,
with stout rubber balls for breasts.
It is difficult to refuse her caress,
dry from the lips her brackish aftertaste,
forget her sweet bitterness.
Underneath her waters wails a rosary of dead
centaurs, watchmen of the shadows.
Handsome men, hard as anchors torn
from the chest of a barbarian god.

It is difficult to refuse the call
of the sea, cover one's ears,
grasp the neck with both hands
and become suddenly mute, or pluck out one's eyes
and feed them to the fish. To ignore the gulls
and red masts and so many pennants,
and the ships arriving from unknown countries
and the ships departing for others
barely known, or perhaps for ours.

Because we carry within
like a blue keel or masts and spars
the marine bitterness of kelp,
the stripes on the back of fishes,
the tarry death
and our initials written in the sea.

Brother moving away to the bridge
like one more piece of our island,
the sea of mariners, your bride.
You know the smell of death
because you tread beneath a cemetery
that can be yours and you go brightly.

You know how the sea smells of life,
how at times she spits a ferocious foam,
how she wails wild and rises
like an atavistic being, a primitive creature.

We all carry death within written in furrows
like a name traced by the keel
of your boat in the sea. We are all sailors
of a sleeping bride with round breasts.

I don't want to depart for the land,
to sprout like a eucalyptus branch
my eyes blinded by grass.
Wait for me, brother, when you anchor
your vessel in the sea you've loved.
No need to depart so alone, mariner
brother of a seaman gripped
by the earth's open jaws.

ODA A UN JOVEN MARINO
~ José Manuel Cardona

a mi hermano Manuel

El mar es una novia con los brazos abiertos,
con los pechos macizos como balas de goma.
Es difícil negarse a su caricia,
secarse de los labios su regusto salobre,
olvidar su amargor azucarado.
Bajo sus aguas gime un rosario de muertos
centauros veladores de las sombras.
Hombres hermosos, duros, como anclas arrancadas
del pecho de un dios bárbaro.

Ed didícil negarse a la llamada
del mar, taparse los oídos,
agarrar con las dos manos el cuello
y enmudecer de súbito, o arrancarse los ojos
y darlos a los peces. Ignorar las gaviotas
y los mástiles rojos y tantas banderolas,
y los barcos que llegan de países ignotos
y los barcos que parten para otros países
que apenas se conocen, o quizá para el nuestro.

Porque nosotros llevamos adentro
como una quilla azul o arboladura
el amargor marino de las algas,
las barras sobre el dorso de los peces,
la muerte alquitranada
y nuestras iniciales escritas en el mar.

La mar de los marinos, vuestra noviaa
hermano que te alejas sobre el Puente
como un pedazo más de nesutra isla.
Tú sabes el olor que huele a la muerte
porque pisas debajo un cementerio
que puede ser el tuyo y vas alegre.

Tú sabes como huele el mar a vida,
como vomita a veces fiera espuma,
como salvaje gime y se rebela
igual que un ser atávico, criatura primitiva.

Llevamos todos dentro la muerte escrita a surcos
como un nombre trazado por la quilla
de tu barco en el mar. Somos todos marinos
de una novia dormida con los pechos redondos.

Yo no quiero partir para la tierra,
brotar como una rama de eucalipto
con los ojos cegados por la hierba.
Espérame tú, hermano, cuando ancles tu nave
en la mar que has amado.
No has de partir tan solo, mariner
hermano de un marino atenazado
por las fauces abiertas de la tierra.

NIGHTS WITH
~ Andrea Cohen

Nights with carcasses teach you
who you are and aren't: lucky

you are not the calf your half-hour
must debone, nor the night

manager who delights in inviting
a knife to tease the new girl's shirt.

You're not the night or the carcass,
but the man who sees through them,

into the next room, which is a pasture
where the night manager in a corner

stands and writes *I'm sorry* in the damp
air until he means it and the night

vanishes and the carcasses come
back to life and nurse the flesh

wounds of the new girl and her
unblemished flesh too. They tell

her: *it could have been worse*, and
even when night comes, it isn't.

FUNKY STUFF
~ Michael Collier

For a dead guy you looked pretty good,
not only because your t-shirt was clean
and you'd lost some weight but your faded tattoo
had been brightened beyond newness, restored
like the Sistine Chapel, and the acne divots
along your neck and cheek had been filled in
and even the de-oxygenated, liver-color
of your skin had pinked-up, so I thought
maybe the afterlife, which you never believed in,
was like Purgatory, a place you got your body
ready for the limbo party of Paradise,
but because this was a dream,
we were in a high-ceilinged attic, and you
who had never hoarded anything, had filled
the space with piles of clothes, magazines
and newspapers stacked like pillars,
columns of books still in their shrink wrap.
Here and there were clumps of rubber gloves—
black, orange, lavender, and yellow—for what
you called "the funky stuff." I asked, "What's
the funky stuff?" And you said, "I don't know,
but no one wants to touch it."

A ROOM AT AN INN IN NEW ENGLAND
~ Billy Collins

So cold
even with the windows shut
and the weighty drapes overlapping

I thought this is no room
I am lying in,
rather the tomb of a dead radiator

that was buried long ago
according to ancient custom
along with all its things—

the dresser, that chair,
a framed drawing of a duck,
as well as me somehow

under a thin blanket,
my last few breaths
visible in the frigid air,

trying to remember
how the radiator
and I could possibly have met.

HURT
~ Martha Collins

little wound pricked

nerve soul-itch felt

someone else but only

self lengthened picked

deeper dug the wound

licked it like a small

dog companion com-

forting it let me let

me off or off the at the

next and into the sheets

of rain paper blank

god perhaps passing

through the paper rain on

my life my little soul-skin

MICHAELANGELO, *DAVID*, STUDY TWO
~ Peter Cooley

There is a world within the open palm
of my left hand. It dangles by my side.
"Dangles" I said deliberately to sound
awkward, beautiful—spangle and mangle
one word. But when I think of this statue,
my body, longing to identify
with muscularity, fails with a dying fall, and I return to this:
we know the statue stands after we're gone.

My hands can never reclaim the sure grip
I witnessed in my own son at infancy,
the tiny fingers his sure grasp on air,
now at twenty-five supple as they grip
the future we rush toward together,
his the long years open to both his hands,
mine like David's hand, dangling, promising
possibles in my foreshortened moments.

The statue, out of time, its maker thought,
pretends to its own immortality.
This is what statues do we cannot do.

CASSATT, *LYDIA IN A LOGE WEARING A PEARL NECKLACE*
~ Peter Cooley

Mirrors! As if they showed us who we are!
They're here to hold us up for the unseen
behind us, either side, above, below.

Her sister—pearls, fan, pink diagonals,
her dress and matching skin, matching make-up—
almost too made-up for a second glance

until—follow me?—we notice how she's posed.
Behind her in their box, spectators,
the dabs of black for males, females pastels.

She's staring in a mirror, the loge tiers
her background, are all in front of her
I come to Cassatt for these mysteries.

I crave these rearrangements in myself.
I'll let critics dote on the red loge seats.

THE GREAT CHAIN OF BEING
~ Steven Cramer

A Renaissance courtier serenades his lady, her porcelain flesh massed above a stomacher, his Venetian breeches expansive as Philip Sidney on the virtues of artifice. What else can be guessed about the lady's figure rhymes with the shape of her gentleman's mandolin. She sits on a mossy knoll; his smile is Latinate.

The spirals of their matching ringlets;
his velvet pumps pinked with tiny holes;
her delicate pinsons—or are they pincnets?
the two trees branching over them, which touch to make an arch,
>   like a couple dancing the Allemande, a metaphor for the rational
>   Universe.

If you want visual proof of their place on the Great Chain of Being, you'll find them in an attic I'm not sure exists anymore. You'll have to climb stairs steep as a ladder, and rummage through dusty boxes for the remains of the china set, *circa* 1950s or '60s, on which they'll still be courting. Between each chipped and washed-out piece: a sheet from the *Times* or the *Star Ledger*. Even after half a century, a headline like *Man Walks on Moon* may still come as a shock.

IN THE PORCELAIN ROOM 1
~ Cynthia Cruz

Marguerite Duras is showing me
the scars behind the wall.
the juju within the fold.

What is this music, she asks.

In a headdress of bright
red flowers and vine

she is still a child.
in her gold
lamé heels, her pale
cheeks, smeared
red.

Porcelain shimmering
broken and glorious.

*Hold my hand
reader,*

Clarice Lispector
whispers.

We are on the raft
of dead women.

IN THE PORCELAIN ROOM 2
~ Cynthia Cruz

The water sluices beneath us.

A whisper, of a feral animal or an orphan's
final cry.

We are moving toward the end
of everything.

We are heading toward
the city.

It is on fire.

We are going to retrieve
the corpse of our dead sister.

Naked,
she is

sitting near the phone,
smoking, on the stained bare mattress.

Blood and cuts and fever.

She leans toward the camera
and whispers.

IN THE PORCELAIN ROOM 3
~ Cynthia Cruz

Inside the broken hive
of glass bells and whispers.

Clarice Lispector
whispers.

*The red and black
creature is the dearest.*

Her hands are lost
someplace.

They are covering
the gape of her mouth.

The walls are cemented
in broken cuts of porcelain.

HERON IN THE HEADLIGHTS
~ Lydia Davis

(*Last Sunday*)
—Any wildlife reports?
—Yes, actually! I was driving down this winding road into town and I
saw a great blue heron, right in the middle of the road!
—(*Pause*) Was this near water?
—No, I couldn't see water anywhere. There were woods on both sides
of the road, right up to the road. It was very strange.
—What was it doing?
—It was just standing there.
—Was it eating anything off the road?
—No. Anyway, I think they only eat live fish. You usually see them
standing in water and watching for fish.
—I know. What did you do? Did you stop?
—No, I just slowed down as I got closer. I didn't want to honk and
scare it.
—What did it do?
—Well, it walked away down the road in front of me, at the side of
the road—
—It walked?
—Yes, I think it walked quickly, I don't think it ran. Finally it flew up
a few feet—it had huge wings—and then down into a deep ditch
between the trees and the road. The ditch was very deep. I couldn't
see it down there at all. I was worried about what it would do after
I went by. I was worried that it would go back up into the road.
I don't know what it was doing there. I've never seen them away
from water.
—Maybe there was something wrong with it.

(*This Sunday*)
—Any wildlife reports?
—(*Pause*) Well, did I tell you about the heron I saw in the road?

—Yes, you told me about that. You could write a story about it. You could call it "Heron in the Headlights."

—But it wasn't in my headlights. I didn't have the headlights on. It was in the daytime. (*Pause*) I could call it "Heron in the Middle of the Road."

—But that doesn't have the same alliteration.

—But it wasn't at night. It was in the daytime.

—Writers don't have to tell the truth.

—But actually, I could call it that, and then say the headlights weren't actually on—

—You didn't hear me. I said writers don't have to be honest. I was being provocative.

—That's not provocative. I mean—

—Oh. (*Laughs*)

—I know writers don't have to be honest. I could call it "Heron in the Headlights" anyway, and then explain that actually it was in the daytime.

ADULTERY
~ Kwame Dawes

after Troy Maxson in August Wilson's *Fence*

Seasons come and go, you can feel
the heaviness of time in your thighs,
the limp in the ankles, the knees
giving way; when you see stairs
you pause; then climb gingerly,
waiting for the sharp stab of pain;
nothing grand, just the way a body
betrays you; the way clothes fail
you, a shirt clinging where once
you remember the give, the flow
of fabric against skin. Used to be
what you said was quiet understatement,
the secret of deprecation; make
a woman wonder, but you know
that afterward, panting, her body
curled up into itself, her voice
of wonderment will know,
Sweet, Jesus, you spoiled me
forever now, forever, the way
she gets up and puts food before
you, the way she says her name
like water flowing, the softening
of her, the tender freshly in her. Now
you boast bombastic, slapping
the knee, carrying in you only
memory because you know
there is nothing left in you,
nothing you can do; your body
a complex of failure. Every

morning you wake with a stone
in your crotch, the remnant
of youth; when you feel
the pulse of stretched flesh,
the readiness, and there are no
adoring hips to welcome
you, no amazed pleasure at this
feat; it passes with the sound of birds,
flattens to nothing—another waste.
It is this passing of possibility,
this thing wasted by time; it is
the knowledge that tomorrow
you will look back and long for
that hunger in your flesh,
but find only the dull silence
of your loss. It is this
that makes a man drift in search
of open fields, soil ripe for his last
seed; soil waiting, turned greedy
to consume him; the surprise
of new desire, the music
of constant need; it is the way
this flesh shouts its last hurrah
before the airy silence
of an inert crotch, a broken body.

ELEGY FOR A MINOR CHARACTER OF PUCCINI'S
~ Norman Dubie

The red knobs on the heavy furniture are old plums.

The orchestra leader is cleaning his boots
with black dirt in a diagonal moonlight.

The lunar shadows are folded by the father
in the bottom bureau drawer.
A pocket watch like a raw and sunken egg, dropped
into a purple blouse
also folded like the flag
on an alien coffin.

It is just before dawn
and the government is lost in interview
and the firing squad has instead
a live ammunition in the white culled chambers
of the Roman dawn
where a thousand birds lift from the river
just seconds before the report of the guns....

The scribbled note desperately formed
explains it was not the blank
false morning of execution
that disturbed the birds
but the sun saying to someone
maybe this is the happy arrangement
in which finally you too are undone.

MRS. CAVENDISH, HOPE, AND OTHER FOUR-LETTER WORDS
~ Stephen Dunn

Mrs. Cavendish, let's continue, out of habit, to expect
from death a tiny leniency, and when it arrives
let's see if we can choose the transport of our choice.
Not an airplane, of course, but something that might
descend at a speed slow enough to keep us
from what can spoil the illusion of a good time.
Maybe even a vehicle that doesn't move.

But let's not count on it.
Hope, Mrs. Cavendish, is a four-letter word.
Have a little fun, that's all. Wear your hair
in Medusa curls, and turn a few onlookers into stone.
Or like a caterpillar begin to undress, do a little
twirl and a shrug, and emerge as something else.
In the meantime, I'll stay around, an itch in my heart,
sleeping in a different room. Hope it. Hope it all.

TALKING WITH FRANK O'HARA
~ Lynn Emanuel

"Frank," I say,

"the dead, those doorstops, are fine by me,"
and turn the gas so low my poem almost gutters out.

Still, in the landscape,
a red flame glints—

a fleck of flesh.

"But poetry is zippy," Frank exclaims.
"What is it with you

and the downbeat?"

We are staring at the sunset
bulging against the window.

And at the crows.
We love the crows—

the dark snout of them among the trees.
So ungainly, so light, they are scattered

all over the yard, clinkers. Cold coals.
Here, poetry is not too easy

as most things are
the dull particulars of Mirror Street

one beside the other.
We drink and smoke.

I quote Frank to Frank: "I miss myself," I say,

because this morning, pawing through his poems,
Manhattan came back to me like a heart attack.

I miss that saturnine, bookish, sexy,
fragment of a bedroom on West 10th

its windows filled with the maple's
leafy reach, the creak and lurch of swings, the bicyclettes.

I was so intelligent and lonely
stuck up there under the dark eaves of my mind....

"And what," I demand, " happened to those years of art and sorrow?
To the misfortunes of Kline, and Pollock, and Peter Beck

and the man who whispered in the keyhole
"Frank is dead"

and the way half New York sank down and wept?"

A flock of crows reels past, cindery and remote.
"Poetry is a bat out of hell," says Frank.

It's YOU and US and THEM
~ Sylva Fischerová, translated by the author,
Joshua Mensch and A. J. Hauner

who built the jails.
Bloody ketchup and silence blossomed.
Although they reaped a lie,
they had sowed belief,
these lovers of Mary the Liberty, Magdalene the Equality.
Then, only loving Magdalene, who led them
to a fenced plot of land

in Siberia, where Osip Mandelstam used to ask Nadezhda
Mandelstam, while in exile:
„What makes you think you have to be happy?"
and she didn't know what to say
– an exile:
the liberty of a circle
the freedom of an ant –

During mass, the priest says:
An evil which keeps us from loving one another and being happy.

„What makes you think you have to be happy?"
Osip asked Nadezhda,
history flowing by, bones & brains &
consciousness getting choped up,
we,
in a society of prefab anything/everything
don't dry the ad for rain,
looking for broth, but instead—
find froth:
liver kidneys heart,
soul and spirit get hit hit hit

—the liberty of a circle
the freedom of an ant,
and God gets hit hit—

To devote ourselves to something so fully
we don't have room for more!

THE OLD TOWN
~ Luigi Fontanella, translated by Luigi Bonaffini

Late evening at the old village pub
I walk past four deaf-mutes
in the small square time got encrusted
on the twisted sheet metal of the cars
abandoned in Jim's yard
you see them talking to each other in the autumn
wind, lord of every crack
the light from the only street lamp pours
its yellowish dribble onto the pavement
a little while ago a wild-eyed scarecrow came out of the pub
he walked like someone who had gambled everything away
I look at the few closed stores and the old Chinese man on the corner
who persists in spattering around
in the smokegrease of his shanty
for one last customer
who won't come.
The sea air chafes your face
and yet it's still not late
it's still not late.

Further off the little traffic light
marks the last edge of the village
it sways like a one-eyed kite
that kills at random
the way the screeching seagull
whirled in front of me yesterday afternoon
its beak piercing the back
of the crab that was still
moving its legs
I followed it with my eyes as far as I could.
And in the darkness I imagined eyes fastened

to the windows of the houses lying on a precipice above the sea. And yet
it's not late. It's still not late.

Petra dares the night and this evening like every evening
it still keeps the secret
of a mother who lost her son
on a day when he went to the beach
and never came back. He vanished, like Ramiro,
swallowed forever in the sea in space in the darkness
in the sky in its mystery. I too
lived here, I too touched
these stones once, questioning them
feeling them seeking their treasure. Stones
that have survived the blood
and the tears, bitter and oblivious stones,
sold to the first comer stones
that someone hauled on his shoulders
morning after morning without being able
to finish the job. Emma would show everyone
the trapdoor that led from the bedroom
to a small cavern
beneath the house, so many times I would have liked
to climb down there in the darkest darkness ... a sudden
violent gust of wind makes the chain clang
in the well where once
someone drew water for Petra. The chain rattles
hard it knocks mercilessly
but it's still not late,
it's still not late.

The Queen of Azaleas has gone away forever
tonight the wind flays the stones and this grass

that she never grew tired of hardening
and populating with new plants dug up who knows where
and other inventions while
the dogwood tree generously
announced its spotless flowers
every spring. The Queen has gone away
without leaving her new address
along with her dreams of water and of earth
the smell of the little fireplace has vanished
vanished is the calamint picked
one summer afternoon on Shelter Island
vanished too are the two cats found by chance
around Lindenhurst.

Already earth already grass I press my face to the grass
one evening old Amy next door hid
under a pile of dry leaves
from her grandchildren who were looking
for her in vain
and that evening she lost her patience
and suddenly sprang up from the heap of leaves
railing at them. *Clang clang clang*
the well chain resounds brutally
it pushes me beyond
on the couch there are some old newspapers
and magazines still wrapped in plastic
piled haphazardly the girl at the newsstand
was careful to put aside
things the regular customers asked for
one day she introduced me to her husband Tom Hass
at six foot six the poor guy was embarrassed
by his own height ("Will you be staying long
in our village?" and "How do you like it here?")

We are all dead and the parched street muffles
every sound. As in a silent film I watch
the four boys passing the ball to one another
but it's still not late it's still not late.

The author and the translator wish to thank Michael Palma for his helpful suggestions.

THIRD & GALENA
~ Stuart Friebert

in memory of Herb Blau

The Italians were Dagos, the French Frogs,
we were plain old Yids, and the Polish Umpkes
supplied us all with their cabbage rolls stuffed
with meat and rice, especially Augie's mom's.

After he'd muss me up for stealing just 1 pack
of Wings from my pop's drugstore, he'd let me
have a drag and touch the Capt. Richard Bong
card from the back of the pack, claiming he was

our first Ace of Polish descent, and you wouldn't
want to disagree, so I got to eat over at his house
again, where we'd polish off galumpkis as if they
were so many Twinkies and Mrs. Malowski sent

me home with a dozen more. Augie's dead & gone
now, so there's no reason to attend another reunion,
the only times I could beat him at arm wrestling. He
knew by then Bong was of Swedish descent, but I

didn't rub it in. After too many brews, we'd slip out
into the alley behind school, walk into the hollyhock
patch, pull out Camels, poor cousins of Wings, we
joked. Augie still carried Bong's card in his wallet,

which we'd salute before heading back for the last of
the festivities, at which point the emcee, usually Freddie
Friedman, would have the spotlight directed at us, shout,
"There's America for you, folks, a Yid and an Umpke,

still friends no matter what!" Augie started coughing,
and I'd join him for solidarity until his lungs stopped
working, he'd stagger, all grew dark, something fell,
and the Chinese lanterns couldn't keep the light alive.

CLOUD OF KNOWING
~ Philip Fried

God's a committed statistician,
An acolyte of decision science,
Intent on minimizing risk,
Constantly seeking optimization,
Cognizant of each fallen sparrow,
The regrettable fact of collateral damage,
But figuring outcomes for the flock.

With his green plastic gambler's visor—
A nod to nostalgia's not amiss,
A wink at the old theory of forms—
In a room as far from Plato's cave
As warmer-toned fluorescence can take him,
Cocooned by arrays of supercomputers
Galloping at an exaflop rate,
With a single index finger, he inputs
Commands for drones named for archangels.

Anyway, a cave's down below
Somewhere, while he's in a floating, nowhere
Cloud....
        Often, he'll don a big pair of headphones
To tune in on, and monitor,
The earthly chatter from everywhere.

COUNTING ORGASMS*
~ Jeff Friedman

My lover counts her orgasms.
It gives her something to do
during sex
besides have orgasms.
She closes her eyes, and the numbers
follow, first evenly, then
in great bursts. Sometimes
I simply blow
gently into her as if
pursing my lips on a velvety reed
and playing a melancholy melody.
And sometimes I use a little chocolate
on my tongue or some Bali Rose
jelly on my fingertips,
rubbing them against her fur,
orchids, long pink ribbons, red grapes.
And my lover cues me
between the numbers,
a little more of this, a little
less of that as if adapting a recipe
from the *NY Times* cooking section.

*

My lover appears in a Nin Andrews poem.
A world-beater,
she's the nameless woman
who once counted 27 orgasms.
Nin imagines 27 penises—
penises like tulips or rabbits,
pale pink and soft, but my penis

is no tulip or rabbit;
no pearly handled tool
uncanny in its precision;
it's an intrepid traveler
trekking and camping.
The day my lover counted 27 orgasms,
I counted only 23.
I marked down each orgasm
on a pad of paper—
like flashes of light
on a dark wall or truffles
wrapped neatly in red foil.
When she gave me her tally,
I nodded in agreement and added
four more marks to the page.

*

My lover is counting again
so I lift my head for a moment.
Sometimes I think she's faking
a few or counting
a shiver or a minor shudder
when it really isn't,
but who can map
the boundaries of an orgasm
when each orgasm maps
its own boundaries or charts
its own vital signs, its own
crests and troughs. Sometimes
when she starts counting,
I leave the room
and get a piece of fruit
or look out the window

to see if I can spot a coyote
in the darkness. When I come back,
she's still in ecstasy
or else fighting her way out
of a bad dream waiting
for me to hold her,
and whisper in her ear, it's okay.

MOLE PEOPLE
~ Carol Frost

Leeches, slugs, flatworms, beetles, centipedes,
feral cats and dogs, and the cold flames
mole people in city tunnels awaken to.
Ignis fatus, luces del tesoro,
the stories tell, and who isn't a scavenger
of stories? For some the moles are lost
souls, for others Hell's embers help
find their bearings. Below squander,
mole people make their lives, receding as night
recedes, advancing in pitch-black
along lost stream beds, climbing the grates
and into metal dumpsters where
every necessity can be carried underground.
One moleman found a book case,
yet I wonder if I were inside his head
would I be reading as the moleman or as me?
The sensitivity of my hand
is six times poorer than the star
of the star-nosed mole, and to imagine
its tactile world, all my perception
must be as if my body were all finger and tongue.
But I have little desire to leave
the colorful and airy streets
and cannot imagine myself touching
an arm of the man whose coat is inside out.
The lights in the marshes, it is said,
will follow you but stand still if you stand.

EQUAL TO THESE FLOWERS
~ Forrest Gander

Such moments he marks,
recalling them to his son—as when
they sledded Suicide Hill and spilled
from the sled, the boy landing on top
of his father who slid in his slick down
jacket down the hill on his back
clutching his son, the both of them
wheezing with laughter—
freeze into set pieces through the father's
reportage and are finally, for him, far
less affecting than what
goes unmeasured and floats
around him with motes
of dust. Ordinary and unsorted.

THE DEAD WOMAN'S TELEPHONE
~ Amy Gerstler

"Hello, I'm Jewish,"
is a playful way
to answer the dead
woman's telephone.
What happened to all
the Jews in Poland?
demands a gravelly
voice on the dead
woman's telephone.
Should one wear
a poppy in one's lapel
when placing a call
from the dead
woman's telephone?
Voicemail retrieved
from the dead
woman's telephone:
Yes yes, the Jews.
We were sorry
to see them go.
They made rose petal
marmalade. They gave
babies poppy seed tea
to make them sleepy.
The rumble of pogroms
is heard while falling
asleep, ear resting
on the receiver
of the dead
woman's telephone.
Light sluices

into the room as a
female police officer,
on the ninth or tenth
ring, picks up the dead
woman's telephone
and jerks open her
curtains. You must be
resolutely on the side
of the lowly
to hear all that's said
on the dead
woman's telephone.
Proposals
concerning relocation
of the forsaken
are now being received
via the dead
woman's telephone.

SWIMMING TO NEW ZEALAND
~ Douglas Goetsch

Once or twice in life you find a woman
you'd swim the ocean for. *What are you doing?*
friends will ask, as you perfect your stroke,
meantime pitying everyone outside of love.
Your only obstacle, the blue Pacific—
where your sun sinks, she's dressing in the morning,
and when the dawn comes reaching back around
bringing the lights back up on your city,
she's drawing blinds, removing her make-up.
If you were Gatsby you would build a mansion
in some cove off the Tasmanian sea
and throw parties to lure her in. You're not
of course—though nothing's impossible,
except life without her, and so you swim.

MUSIC AT AN EXHUMATION
~ Beckian Fritz Goldberg

This spring they dug up Pablo Neruda to see if he was poisoned.
A guitar, a violin, played beside the grave overlooking the sea,
though what good is a grave that overlooks the sea. Still
the desert blooms a thousand golds and yellows, summoning
every possible memory. Still the moth like a dusty ghost
tries to unbutton the window at night. And I can tell you
on the same night in the east Antares burns like a rose that has seen hell.
It is the night of my 59th birthday, the resinous scent
from sweet acacias drifts the cool dark, and I am asking what happened.
What happened to the Bulgarian who gave me ten dollars once
when I was young and desperate for bus fare home. What happened
to Mrs. Biggs in the fourth grade who'd warn me before she read
the sad part of a story. What happened to the first boy who kissed me.
What happened to my father. It is a time of wonder—
Neruda has flown to Santiago. They have X-rayed his body
and studied the images. A wine jug hung from a tree. The sacra's
eaten face. What happened to Kathleen—the girl I discussed my first
kiss with, the girl I smoked my first dope with and the girl who called
years later when her marriage was unraveling but by then I was bound by
my own misery and could help no one. What happened to
my friend South Carolina who I met in jail. What happened to everyone?
All day the wind has blown and I'm tired of it. It blew
a dead bird onto my patio. A flicker. One day you're driving
home from work and it comes to you you haven't seen that cashier
with the thick spectacles at the supermarket in a while. Maybe he
got fired. Maybe he got a better job than ringing up
canned goods all day long. Me? I'm just trying get a dead bird
up with a shovel and then I don't know where to carry him. Tonight
the air is heavy with pollen. Everything swollen with resurrection.
The sad part of the story when I was nine was the part where
the dog died and since I already knew the story I told Mrs. Biggs

it was OK and braced myself. Still, I covered my ears until
she looked up and nodded. Still, I remember the name of the dog
was Jack, that they buried him in the prairie and later
moved away. Some things kill you every time. When you look up
it is spring again and some tough Camaro, woofers booming
from the trunk, vibrates in your breastbone with its stronger heartbeat.
There are no lights along the road until the city limits. I listen
as the throb goes soft with distance and the desert's flat quiet again.
It is late; nothing can happen now. No one ever dreams
they will be fifty-nine, that spring has come fifty-nine times
and fifty-nine blossoms in the acacia, sweet as laundered sheets,

tannic as tobacco, perfume the blind air where they have lost track.
It was just last week the Venezuelan government announced
plans to exhume Hugo Chavez to see if he'd been deliberately
infected with cancer. This same man who had them bring up
the bones of Simon Bolivar so he could converse with them.
Is the whole of South America crazy? Is it crazier than North America
where no one mentions death except those who don't believe in it,
the body a mere burden to be discarded, gently, in the brush of the
    arroyo
by someone with a shovel—is it crazier than heaven? What happened
to the crazy kid from the halfway house who kept sending me his
    paintings
because I'd been nice to him when I taught night school English.
They were a gibberish of color on cheap canvas board. Most of them
looked like they were on fire though sometimes there were pencil
figures with round heads and sometimes buildings with windows
behind the paint. I kept them in the closet mainly as evidence
for I was positive he was going to murder me. But after five years
the paintings stopped coming, and he has let me live at least
to fifty-nine which somehow seems as ancient to me as it did when
I was sixteen. Night still smells of creosote. The first stars smart

from the blue blackness. Say
the painter of those paintings came back and murdered me, don't
    come back
years later and raise me from the ground to prove it. There comes
a time when the body no longer desires to be seen, it is done being,
unrecognizable even to itself had it an eye left. It's purpose
was always beauty, not justice. All that is left of Neruda is bone.
Doctors extract some marrow and send it to North Carolina
for tests. I have died fifty-nine times
of spring. I have fifty-nine times rehearsed myself as ghost. I have been
    a figure
drawn in pencil behind the flames. What happened to me? What
happened to the night that drove past fields of blind sugar beets, past
the electric castle of the power station, into the desert, did it
ever stop? What happened to Edgar Poe? I once climbed over
the churchyard's iron fence to leave a bud on his grave, and also
a tube of lipstick, deep cerise, should he rise some evening and haunt
the misty docks of Baltimore with the need to feel desire, with
the need for a mouth. In truth, we die of nothing else. In truth
we die the moment we love. In truth, you kill me with your face.
Not so long ago, the Italians opened Petrarch's tomb to take his skull
and reconstruct his face but they found in it a man's body
and the shattered skull of a woman. Someone had stolen the left arm.
Perhaps his eyes were deep set and dark as spring night,
miro pensoso le crudeli stelle, che m'ànno facto di sensibil terra—
I gaze pensively at cruel stars that have created me of sentient earth.
This night smelling of incense and iron, blind with thought. This *not.*
Neruda is not Neruda. The night drags its violet hair. Your face is not
your face. Think of the man who stole Petrarch's head, was he not
like us—raising an empty lantern as if what was once there
still flamed. It is spring. The orange moon arrives like a painting.
Why did you die? Why did you die and leave me shapeless
with 59 holes, with 59 letters in the alphabet. And Pablo Neruda
poisoned. Pablo, I knew that crazy kid was in love with me

and I could not stop it. I could not stop my body from appearing
in his mind. From lighting 59 fires. *Miro pensoso le crudeli stelle* ...
In his last painting I thought I saw a window far in the orange yellow,
the flames shaped like golden hysterical women, the soft green-hackled
sprites of space, and understood why he might pour gasoline
around an empty house one night and light a match, why when
the cops came he might still be standing outside with his gas can
watching form eat form. It was felony transcendence. That far gold
      window
extinguished in the back of the closet behind the sad-sleeved coat I
      never wore.
These nights, half-cool, I stand outside the house—as if I'm waiting
but for what I couldn't say. When they dug up Allende, two springs ago,
they examined the hole left by the AK47 he'd held under his chin
and confirmed the cause of death was suicide. All the arms in the earth,
all the teeth, hips, ears and knees in the earth, yield us nothing. The
      body
has told us all it knows which first and last is separation. Between,
hunger, heat, habit, heavenly touch, helplessness, beauty and
more beauty and more hurt—like music at an exhumation
it is the difference between a silence, and a violin and then a silence.
Still the desert blooms a thousand golds and yellows which are steeped
      in night
and exude memory. Still the ashy moth falls open to the same page with
its mysterious watermark. And spring rises from the underworld alone
and dies of nothing.

CRIPPLE CREEK
~ Arielle Greenberg

We "dropped out,"
but yellow lights outside the bedroom window again tonight.
Cops or the snowplows.

The oil furnace beneath us,
churning like an egg.
We keep it quite cold,
but the winter air is colder still.
A sense of the pioneer about things.

I.e., a wild place for being free
and in love in the country.
Small criminal acts and roadkill.

     In the parking lot of Reny's,
     two white-haired women, serious Buddhists
     buying discount trash bags,
     stop to talk to me about the poems I read
     at the American Legion the month before.

     A letter arrives for our daughter
     addressed to just her name and the street's,
     no house number.
     In these ways we are already known.

There are places about which you say
"I'm going up," like a pilgrimage, an ascending.

THE STORY WRITER
~ Jeffrey Greene

in memory of Mavis Gallant

North light, half-curtained, the room
where nothing happens, a book is read,
dark tea cools, a pen travels thin rails
to the horizon, the margin of a tablet.
The characters talk, they always do
and their meaning is clear though
the words themselves were still forming
on their tongues, the tone chosen
like a flavor, and they are almost
like people we know, even more so,
their age, clothes, religion, dreams.
Of course, someone is deeply hurt,
someone always is, but now these
circumstances barely show it.

AUTOCHROME
~ Kelle Groom

She's gold-ringed as if a child bride.
Lap of apples, eyes elsewhere.
Institutionalized sixty-four years.
At the beginning of the last century,
the treatment was long baths,
barbiturates. *She stared into*

a photograph calling for her father.
When her son was born, she was diagnosed
with *post partum dementia praecox*,

considered an incurable disease.
To manifest, show oneself, appear.
No one says it anymore.

The Scottish *kythe*: make visible.
Kithe also Old English, to make known,
reveal. She's placed inside the black box

of a diascope which reveals her in a mirror.
In glass held to light, or projected.
Reversed—negative to positive—

she appears as she really is.
To make her visible, potato starch was dyed,
four million microscopic grains.

Gold chain bracelet half fallen
on the white sleeve of her dress, though
everything that isn't dark is light

violet. Mouth an answering curve,
palm another.
Sun hat planetary over brows,

her eyes look inward, away.
She holds her chin
in the palm of a hand younger

than her face, still cushioned.
Wrecked by wars and weather,
all kinds of breakage,

autochromes are rare.
The first true color photographs
black glass.

THE DEATH ROW DREAM
~ Rachel Hadas

This latest iteration: I was given
an index card on which to jot last thoughts.
But what to write, and to whom to write it?
There were no chairs. We three in a dim hall,
mini-skirted, leaned against the wall.
Heavy maroon curtains barely stirred.
Hours passed: no resolution.
And woke back into human time, its mercy,
its stern redistribution.

FROM *TOYING*
~ Kimiko Hahn

[Unlike *Tiddlywinks*]

Unlike *Tiddlywinks*, I do not move if pressed. Especially by a squidger. Like *Tiddlywinks*, I am strategic (develop, maintain, break—i.e., DMB). Especially squopping an opponent, especially after I turned thirty and did not feel compelled to tolerate winks and such. I do, however, delight in feeling felt.

[Like *Mouse Trap*]

Like *Mouse Trap*, I can keep my little trap shut. Almost exclusively when it comes to girlfriends' ailments or affairs. Not so much my own. So don't call me *mousey*.

[Like *Operation*]

Like *Operation*, I pretty much feel alarmed most of the time—not that one would notice. Unlike *Operation*, my alarm is not a signal of pain so much as traumatic residue: hair-pulling, cellphone games, and the obsessive like. Anyway, like *Operation*, I too can test another's dexterity—but *sans* battery! And tweezers are my best friend though not for a charlie-horse!

[Like *Chatty Cathy*]

Unlike my best friend, I did not have a *Chatty Cathy*. Unlike my best friend, I did have a little sister who basically never stopped chattering. I wondered how she never stopped, especially on road trips, and wished that she had a chatty-ring sticking out from her back! Oh, I so wanted a *Chatty Cathy* but my parents just saw a breakable mechanism. Now I'm not so sure it was good to have a doll that chirped, "Please take me home with you!"

CZARINA ALEXANDRA MEETS LENIN IN HELL
~ Barbara Hamby

I'm not here. I was devout, loved my husband, who was a weak man I will admit, but I gave him a son and four beautiful daughters, though Tatiana was my favorite, so lovely, like looking into a mirror and seeing myself as a girl. But to be here with you. Let me speak to God, there must be some explanation.

We both loved Beethoven, but I can't see that listening to the *Appassionata* could damn one to hell. "Murder?" you say. I never killed a living thing; well, maybe a fly or mosquito, but there were servants who did that. I have no blood on my hands.

And your beloved proletariat, one of those animals put a finger inside me while they were dragging our bodies to the hole where they buried us. Of course, I was dead, but my body was my body.

ACCIDENTS WILL HAPPEN
~ Bob Hicok

A table. I wanted to make a table.
For books to sit on. I'd thought
table table table for weeks.
But when I picked up the wood,
when I marked, when I cut, a tree
came out. I made a tree
out of what had been a tree.
And took the tree inside.
And tried to put a book
in the tree but the tree said no,
the tree wanted a bird, the tree
was a traditionalist. It reminded me
of the time I thought I was going
to a dinner party but fell in love
with my wife before she was my wife.
When she was just a woman
in t-shirt and jeans
coming around a corner to claim
her share of the asparagus.
I got the tree its bird. In getting
the tree its bird, I got us singing
we didn't know would make the ceiling
resemble the sky. Especially
where we painted it blue.
All over. Even in the hard
to reach places. Right under
our skulls, where no light goes.

So, Bacteria Also Have Their Thunder
~ Brenda Hillman

           & cloud caps
    in the drought—   microbes
on the leg of   the wild cat,   specks
      on its   photo—in *nature*,   buckles near
grasses   of perhaps   not growing …
no rain this week,   no relief sounds …   in our grief
here,   to hear   coastal cypress—   beware—
    so grown things   rain:
between life & nonlife &
       death: the whir
under the dove's wing, to—rows of marigolds,

    an end of earth   where creatures go
without supervision … such
      sorrow i heard—
    such sorrow they heard …   bacteria
also have their thunder   in the nightlight
   of the biome,   coasting,   coastal
      outside an arrogant   noise
they never made   — breaks
   energy   in   sun's
      setting   behind a band
of   thunder clouds: cracks & volunteers—

A PHOTOGRAPH OF A FACE HALF LIT, HALF IN DARKNESS
~ Jane Hirshfield

Even 3 + 2 is like this.

A photograph of a face half lit, half in darkness.

A train station where one train is stopped
and another passes behind it,
heard, but not seen.

A person proud of five good senses
lives without echolocation.

Dogs pity our noses
as we pity the bee that blunders the glass.

Take out every other word of the world,
what is left?

A half half darkness.

A station one is and passes.

We live our lives in one place
and look in every moment into another.

As on a child's map,
where X
marks both riddle and treasure.

It is near, but not here.

EPISTLE OF MOMENTARY GENEROSITY
~ Tony Hoagland

I get a note from James, my enemy, who used to be my friend,
in which he says he misses me,

so I hold the letter in my hand,
and for a moment just appreciate

this kindness that he squeezed out of his heart
right before that muscle clenched again

and tried to make him take it back,
or add a note that said, *You dirty snake,*

You have my Leonard Cohen albums.
And thus are human beings:

not always frightened and unkind. They
have moments when the mind unclouds

and old injuries are forgiven;

when the policeman hands the criminal a cigarette
and they stand in place and smoke, and stare

out the window at the rain;
when the lifejacket is tossed

from the back deck of a ship
too big to turn around—good luck!

That freely given impulse—there it goes.
An hour later, you might regret your

open-handedness, or think it weak,
but it is done, and gone; the blessing

has escaped;
and like a gull it sails

right through the momentary gap,
across the churning ocean,

between the judgment cliffs.

WHAT THEY TOLD ME AT THE BOY'S CLUB IN GAINESVILLE
~ Tony Hoagland

Right over there, in the public library, that's where Rahul got shot—
all engrossed in front of the science fiction shelf, reading *Teenage
   Nymphomaniacs from Mars*

with a studious expression and a moderate erection,
which may be why he got taken by surprise.

They took him downtown in the ambulance, but left the crime scene
      cordoned off
and a pool of blood on the hardwood library floor for evidence,

right under the murder mysteries,
like some kind of promotional display;

And Mrs. Kennedy kept the checkout desk open till nine p.m., out of
      principle,
even though she was frowning and crying the whole two hours,

and making little noises to herself
which in a book might have been described as "muffled cries for help."

And Rahul, who didn't make it all the way to closing time,

died in the corridor of Mercy General,
and left his seventeen-year-old body on the crash cart

with the unused library card in his front shirt pocket,
as he himself was a book that was never carefully read.

To some it signified the need
for more metal detectors;

for others it was definite proof
that reading can be bad for your health

but when the priest at the funeral said that Rahul had gone to a better
     place
we could only hope that it looked nothing like Gainesville, Florida;

and it made us feel better to imagine
that the angels who met and took him there

appeared in the disguise
of teenage nymphomaniacs from Mars.

THE WORLD IS AS PRETTY AS A PICTURE
~ Tony Hoagland

of a wedding in spring,
when the dogwood tree blossoms like a big bouquet
flinging pink and white confetti to the wind.

The world is pretty as a picture
but when you hold up a magnifying glass
you see the best man pissing
on the neighbor's shrubs

and the child just drifting towards the penned-up dog.
You see the make-up on the step-daughter's black eye
and the mother kneeling on the bathroom tile to pray
while the nephew carves a word
                              into the wall.

There are, as Shakespeare said,
the nightingales and vultures.
There are the workers and the loafers.
There are the saints

and then there are the motherfuckers.
And there is something un-
accountable,
something unknown coming into town,
gathering force off to the side,

like a wind
from out beyond the willow tree,
under the strung-up Christmas lights
where the bride is dancing
                              with her ex-boyfriend

and the crazy uncle
is watching
and checking his gun.

EUGENICS
~ T. R. Hummer

An abandoned clinic, empty as if after a war,
    still furnished with chairs of medicinal green,
Desks the color of old photographs, a beveled mirror
    discolored by sunlight, catalyzed with dust.
 In the black light of consciousness, smears
    of blood and semen glow on surfaces
No one would have thought contaminated by any
    trace of human leakage. It is the antechamber
Of a mind disordered by the impure chemistry
    of selfhood. Inside the sealed file drawers,
Row after row of folders, each tab inscribed
    in gold, where the priests stood in their apparel
With trumpets, and the Levites, the sons of Asaph,
    with cymbals, to praise all that has gone
To sediment, oxide, and carbonaceous brume.

SAFETY PIN
~ Mark Irwin

I must have carried it around for 15 years
in my shaving kit, hoping to use it sometime
but never did until one day on a plane this guy
next to me asked if I happened to have a safety pin?
Sure, I said, and stood up to take it out of my luggage.
He'd torn his shirt—no big deal—but it was on the shoulder
where he couldn't reach. I held the pin up like a tiny sword
then went to work, bending toward him as if to whisper
something. "I'm dying," he said, stone-faced.
What, I said. "That's why I'm going to Cleveland, a final
experiment for my shot kidneys." Dialysis? I asked. "For years,"
he said, holding a long cord, looped at both ends
on his lap. He fingered it like a rosary. What's that? I asked.
"It's a bowstring," he said. "I'm an archer." Wow, I said, leaning
back toward him, tucking, re-pinning the tear, then patting
his shoulder. "I started with a toy bow my father gave me,
rubber-tipped arrows and all. Now I've been to tournaments
all over the world," he added, then his head dropped, even though the
        plane
seemed to be climbing as the sun broke through clouds, catching
his body. Slowly I slipped my finger through one loop of
the cord and I pulled and he pulled till it was taut.

CARROLL COUNTY, VIRGINIA
~ Devin Johnston

Stand up, plead my case before the mountains,
let the hills hear what you have to say.
Sum it up for slick and rough so thick
no light or law could penetrate,
only the ringing of an axe
and wagon's creak en route to Fancy Gap.

As I cleared a stand of pine,
no thought but for the task at hand,
the deputy sheriff came along
with my two brothers atop a mule,
one cuffed, the other tied.
Have you got a requisition
to bring those boys across the line?
When he said no, I took his gun,
hit him with the butt
and broke it on a rock.

All that spring, from cove to cove,
the Baldwin-Felts detectives
tried to root us out,
a cold spring, the tracks filled
with apple blossoms and snow.
They finally caught us in a barn
boiling stolen eggs,
our brogans red with mud,
our topcoats stiff as horse collars
and redolent of ramps.

All that spring my cabin stood
unlocked and as I left it,

a water pump not yet installed,
the porch in need of paint.

In court, I wore a borrowed suit,
a toothbrush in my breast pocket,
and tilted my chair against the rail,
dozing in and out of sleep.
I dreamt that Thomas Edison
electrocuted a rat, and then
a hound and then a horse,
filling the air with the acrid smell
of singeing hooves and fur.

When the clerk read out a verdict
and the sheriff fetched his cuffs,
I dropped my chair legs, stood up,
and said, *I ain't a-going.*
That's when the shooting started—
and through the powder smoke and noise
so loud no sound remained distinct,
just as where a waterfall
drowns out every drain and creek,
my brothers and I made for the door
and down the courthouse steps,
leapt across a picket fence,
tossed our pistols in a slick
and lit out for the hills.

ON LOVING TWO MEN AT ONCE
~ Marilyn Kallet

Okay, three. The crooner
  young enough to be
my grandson—who am I,
  Georgia O'Keefe?
The second, son-like,
  son-down, and
bien sûr, my careless,
  dark-eyed
  husband. Whom I
adore. It's harmless, Ladies
  & Gents, long as
all comers remain
  locked in an ode.

While we're ensnared in
  dream light,
why not add the hotel owner's
  son at the Quartier Latin, my
tool-time hero with his
  homemade quickie cardboard boxes,
dark-haired Fabio
  tearing duct tape with
his teeth, while his toddler son,
  rapt, studies him.

On loving four men at once—
  N, S, E, W, let me be
the center of the compass!
  It's part-time love, in a country
of lost souls and souvenirs,
  4/4 time.

Dark-eyed gentlemen
  of my dreams,
I'd say there are none
  like thee among poets
with swift feet,
  but I just tagged a few more.

In the realm of perfect bodies
  & dream light,
of ordinary love,
there's plenty
to go around,
loop-de-loop.

 How do you say "roller coaster"
in French, I asked?
"*Les montagnes russes*,"
Fabio said.
I love you like the
Russian mountains,
up and
down.

THE FACE
~Laura Kasischke

The only other patient here today—
A blonde I saw ten years ago, gone gray.
And why would I recall this woman's face
When so much else I've seen has slipped away?

A total stranger really. Dissolving wall
Between my memory and her and all
The tin toys wound too tight, the funerals—
While she's been locked inside me. I'm a vault!

A dresser drawer! Silk underthings, white lies —
A woman's face. A decade passing while
I tried to hail a cab that just sped by—
And she was in it, staring out, free ride

In someone else's memory. She smiled
And disappeared, it seemed. Married well,
I'm sure. And tended roses. Wrote her novels.
At the center of her wedding cake, a bell

Made out of even sweeter cake. I've tasted
bells myself. In vivid rooms, I've waited
As jellied fruit was passed around, vows taken.
What money buys. What beauty, as it fades—

"I know you," if I knew her, I would say.
But what is she to me now anyway?
A blonde I saw ten years ago, gone gray—
The other patient waiting here today.

The pages of my magazine are thin.
The music of a crow has been piped in.
Nurse, overweight. The doctor's late again.
I find my iPhone in my purse, and then—

Her bald child (a girl, perhaps eleven)
Is wheeled into the room to rest her head
Between her mother's broken heart and broken

Wing. Broken and forgotten, everything.

WINDOWS ON THE WORLD
~ Dore Kiesselbach

Looking for a black tie meant to hang straight,
I see the winged one with its clip I wore
atop the north tower, a law firm party
that made the news for 20K spent
on roses flown from the equator.
It had been a banner year.
The last silk I held
I held against cinders
to my nose and mouth.
Gram by gram it
more than dazzles
steel. The larva gets
a chance to boil *in*
situ without ruining
its cocoon. So high
above steerage, who
would have thought
to pray that nothing
should prevent us
from going down?
When the fog rolled
in like silk the city
shed its wings of light.
When the fog rolled
in like smoke we were
as good as drowned.

ART OF THE LONG WINTER LET 1
~ John Kinsella

Harbinger of global warming
tucked into mountains with a sub-
tropical bent, this Aagaard view of Lake Como:
assured Roman columns and enthusiastic
plant-life, creepers and flowers and urns,
spilling perspectives. High place above
the Industrial Revolution's pits and toxins,
and its present manifestation, the Hadron Collider,
not *too far* away, a deep-earthed villa,
rocking the sublime to its core.

                              In this house
looking out over hedged fields, cows
in their deluded hijinks, green-sloped island
caught in the sun, the bay, and the picture
that would be a painting becalmed over
a peat fireplace (almost decorative, though not quite,
briquettes stacked *just right* will burn with a carbon
residue of deaths and spirits, life's building-blocks),
resonates rustic classicism, a realist hoodwink.
Study its surface with a curatorial nod
to a forger's compulsion, and the rippled
surface is as clear as floor varnish, the poster
a mass-produced irony comfortable
as an auction lot.

                    Shelley would be in bliss
in this Mizen Head house, a new draft
of Queen Mab writing itself, Killarney's
strawberry-treed islands a few hours' drive
and short boat-trip away.

                              This house, let
to summer vacationers when idyll
is what's paid for, eases into functionality
over winter, artwork mocking those
who come in the face of the weather, peer out
into the rain and blurred pastoral images
with restorative energies reserved
for that pinnacle of ontological
and mythical health,
                    Lake Como.

ART OF THE LONG WINTER LET 2
~ John Kinsella

A version of this painting is described by an art reproduction company
As a 'very pretty English Victorian conservatory scene'. There are many
Takes on this template: *this* one includes a cupid with a long-handled
    mirror
And a luscious marble Aphrodite whose nudity you'd rub to a lustre.
There are other singular bespoke items that set off the religious soberness
Of the room and house it is hung in: the pentagonal brass and glass case
Holding a mysterious urn that might enhance the living or the dead,
The Babylonian horseman on his onyx steed marching across the
    battlefield
Of a velvet-clothed table. But the table is standard, backdropped by broad
Warm-climate leaves that will umbrella you from heavy rain or provide
Shade when the sun breaks its hallucinatory bonds and gets deep inside.
The leaves and the flowers, the rich red floor and Persian carpet, crystal
Chandelier and ornate chair, profusion of palms, creepers and spiral-
Lathed legs of plant stands, all vaguely familiar, to be taken in your stride.

THE JUDGMENT OF PARIS
~ David Kirby

This hotel has a lot of Klimt reproductions on its walls,
  and as I look at his smiling naked ladies swimming in a sea
of jewels, I recall the art historian who says that Klimt
    revealed women's inner desires, whereas to me
it looks as though the paintings reveal men's outer desires regarding

women's inner desires, namely, that the women want to have
  sex with the men! This hotel's in Greece, not that far from
the spot where Paris had to give the golden apple to one
    of three goddesses: Hera, who offered
to crown him king, Athena, who assured victory in war, and Aphrodite,

who promised him the world's most beautiful woman. Paris
  was, what, seventeen, eighteen? Too, in all the paintings,
the three goddesses are naked and beautiful themselves,
    meaning Paris was already thinking
of something besides Euclid's proof of the infinitude of prime numbers.

As art critic John Berger says, men look at women,
  and women watch themselves being looked at, that is,
by men, which I assume is what's going on in the song
    where a girl, my lord, in a flatbed
Ford turns around to take a look at you, but it's just as true that women

watch themselves being looked at by other women.
  I mean, obviously Zeus knew he was rigging the contest,
but surely the three goddesses were in on it as well.
    Poor dumb Paris: he accepts Aphrodite's
gift and gives the apple to her. Big mistake. He gets Helen of Sparta,

but she's already married to Menelaus, who isn't amused;
    the result is a war that lasts ten years. Also, Paris pissed
off Hera, aka Mrs. Zeus, whereas he should have
    applied poker theory and played
to her by "extracting maximum value" from a "positive expectation."

Paris never learned one of life's key lessons:
    when the money's gone and the drugs are gone, the girl
is gone. He was never going to keep the face that launched
    a thousand ships and toppled the topless towers
of Ilium. Oh, well. No paradox, no art—no contradiction, no Dante,

Verdi, Virginia Woolf, Puccini, Klimt. Paris would
    probably say he had a good run, though, and inspired
Homer to write both an epic poem with him in it
    and an even better one after that. What is
a good poem? I know, one that makes you want to write a poem yourself.

REDEMPTION
~ Karl Kirchwey

The tenants will not renew:
      the house risks standing empty.
      All the childhood fears come over me,
the moves every year or two,

the family broken as a family,
      the heartsick burden of place
      dragged through continents and cities,
the constant anonymity,

the weird dislocated shame.
      Then, standing before a door painted
      the color of dried blood,
my father appeared in a dream,

who gave me the little he could
      (and for all that, it was enough)
      out of his own fear and love,
he with whom life did what it wanted,

now twenty-five years gone,
      with his limping gait and his game smile,
      both resolute and vulnerable,
wearing a sweater colored fawn

like any hunted thing.
      Impulsively I embraced him:
      his body was solid and warm,
but the air was alive with his perishing,

or rather, it was as if he had put
      the seals on one house, on all houses,
      in which, through a velvet darkness,
motes glittered in a column of sunlight.

Father, when shall I join you in that kingdom,
      as you stand in front of a door
      closed on so much empty air?
And how shall I know it is home?

OUR ROBOTS
~ Jennifer L. Knox

Hal, the robot in *2001*, wants to kill the astronaut.
Forty years later, Gerty, the robot in the movie *Moon*,
wants to save the astronaut. Was *Moon* written by
a robot? No. Maybe Gerty is a nicer robot because
we're getting smarter about robots, smarter without
knowing it. That's how people get smarter: dumbly,
without knowing it, until years after the smart's set in
and we're dumb in whole new ways. It's exciting,
the ways in which we're newly dumb! Robots are
novelties. Without novelties, we'd pull our feathers out.
When the movie robot was invented, we couldn't pull
ourselves away. Some starved in the seats. We died
in front of the TV robot watching quiz show robots,
died bowed down before the warm radio robot with its
shell-shocked boogie-woogie, died guzzling the dark,
dank developing bath of the photograph robot, died
weeping with the lute robot, died screwing around
like punks with gunpowder robots, died carving stars
in stone with chisel robots, wheel robots, fire robots.
Maybe Gerty is a nicer robot because we are nicer
now (too late?) and robots have our faces. How they
follow us like baby ducks, guessing our next robot.
Ancient cave painting robots with our faces. This one
of a buffalo hunt: there we are.

THE ENCHANTED DIVER
~ Yusef Komunyakaa

We backflip from the skiff,
& ease down, down as if falling
into another, or into a deep cloud
of bubbles & weather of the self
where nightmares go, till a flange
catches & holds, married
to King Neptune's daughter.

We drift among the unnamed
& invade a world of annelid,
serpents, & fauna walking
into a cave to a crystal obelisk
& toppled limestone pyramid
as if descending azure columns
on the shoulders of Poseidon.

We sink into each other's reflection
on walls of an underwater museum.
Ancient feeling, ritual, & certainties
are nearly erased from stone reliefs,
& I'm a few feet inside the temple
of Iris, & my fingers ache to touch
any golden thing of Cleopatra's.

I swim eye-level to a sphinx
in a grand square cocked slant
by the gravity of long waiting,
thankful you have anchored me
here, & I see broken mirrors
of the Alexandrian lighthouse
lit by a school of cuttlefish.

I raise my hands to the mask,
my mouth half open, trembling
in the rage of the earth centuries
before. What was God thinking?
Now, I remember, this is how
I first almost died, learning to work
the inglorious fins on my feet.

EAST MEETS WEST
~ Dorianne Laux

> *It's said that Ho Chi Mihn worked at London's Carlton Hotel from 1913 to 1917 where he may have encountered the American actress Mae West.*

On a summer evening they join forces,
Mae in her gown of tears, Ho Chi Minh
in his kitchen apron stained
with duck blood and grease.

She leans over the butcher's block saying,
A hard man is good to find,
and he replies, *I move with all the dignity
of an ancient government official.*

She says, *A man's kiss is his signature.*
He says, *When the prison doors are opened,
the real dragon will fly out.*

This is when she slides her tongue
in his mouth and they fall
on the seal-tile floor like curved knives,
eyes glazed as the bottoms of copper pots.

Mae's breasts rise from her bodice
and he says, *By reading them
again and again finally I was able
to grasp the essential part.*

She touches his thigh and says
*I speak two languages: Body and English.
I've been things and seen places ...*

The Carlton's grand chandelier is still
lighting up their room in the sky, tea leaves
speaking from the bottoms of their cups.

He says, *Love other human beings*
as you would love yourself.
She says, *I never loved another person*
the way I loved myself.

N27P70
~ Hank Lazer

4 / 12 / 14
diamond head

first light

"we perceive according to

each life & its particular pain

light, just as in verbal communication

to make (more) apparent

the governing nothingness

emerging in time

"... then we suddenly have the impression

of a magical lighting

this

from which

WHO KNOWS? THAT LIFELONG QUESTION
~ Sydney Lea

I. HE RISKS A WALK

Between two pock-marked beeches, on a strand of wire
For cows he recalls from childhood, the cruel barbs shine,
Blossoms of brightness. When darkness stoops, Orion
Will shine likewise, as always, among the stars.
He'll nock his arrow, as if to kindle mayhem
Below. For now, the old man thinks of the house,
Where his wife must still feel disquiet. The weather scared them
Last night with sideways rain, which in due course froze.
When he all but trips on a winter-kill, he wonders,
Has he read somewhere of a people who buried their dead
As the grouse in his path is buried, neck and head
Alone protruding, or was that just some old torture?
The grouse's stiffened ruff is lustrous with frost.

The bird had hidden in powder. When it turned to ice,
It sealed the body in. So peculiar a sight
Has stopped the old man cold in this foolish walk.
Today's no day for wandering under trees
Going off around him everywhere, loud as guns—
The clap and crack of bursting limbs and trunks.
Sunbeams garland the forest in silvery beads,
Every branch and bole, both shattered and whole,
A radiant filament. He can't see why
Death looks so brilliant. Its dead eyes rimed and white,
The head might be a flower, or maybe a jewel
Carelessly dropped by somebody roaming here
Where the walker feels his way, the trail so sheer.

ii. He Walks and Stops

His trail so sheer, his knees not what they were,
The walker finds himself
Pausing more often than stepping, and in these lulls–
Although he's tired of memory,
Damnable habit that's been the stuff of his life–
The past creeps up again.

He muses how it's the biggest surprise he's known:
The fact that he's gotten old,
That, for example, he's forced to put a hand
On each of those cobbly knees
And push down hard whenever he needs to step up
Onto even slight swells or rock-forms.

It's what he did, he recalls, on grammar-school stairs,
And then, in adolescence,
Went on to mock the younger boys for doing.
He sees those small ones still,
Their untucked shirts and trousers and untied shoes
Gone muddy out on the playground,

As they pant on the steps, their little mouths agape,
The dread, imperious bell
Reminds them that they're late again. They're late.
The old man also sees
In this red oak grove a few stumps here and there
Of long-gone trees he hewed

Forty years back or more, their wood turned dozey,
Such that he all but pictures
Their turning to air itself were he to kick them,
Although of course he won't,

For fear of losing balance. Imagination,
Vision—it's all he has,

It seems, by which he means the ceaseless function
Of selective memory.
He thinks of war in Syria now, for instance,
And thinks he ought to be thinking
Of that, or of any news his mother described
In his boyhood as "current events,"
Rebuking his idle dreaming. He hears her voice
To this day and can't gainsay it.
Three cord in eight short hours: that's what he'd fell
And cut and split and stack.
Why shouldn't he still be strong? Another surprise.
He walks on fifty feet

And pauses once again. A random gust
Blows in a scent of winter.
He can't identify it, although it's familiar:
He's taken this odor in
For seven decades, but now he wants to ignore it.
He'd rather not be mired,

For even a moment in even the least old question.
Yet how does one look ahead
Or out from here? The prospect appears absurd.
For all of that, he notes
The buds of February tending to purple
The way they've always done,

And he can't help it: he has to conjure spring.
He can't resist somehow.
Is this mere habit too, or might it be
An authentic sense of revival?

He walks a while again and stops again,
Walks on and doesn't know.

III. HE'LL STAY WITH THAT

He doesn't know as he walks,
That two coyotes are mating
Within yards of where he passes,
In that late-growth fir clump northward.

He knows only enough to imagine
They're there. If he passes again
In eight weeks or so, the bitch
Will howl, if she exists.

She'll be guarding her whelps from the walker
Unless or until he moves on.
If she feels fear, she'll hide it.
Ice out on the river

Will have loosened up its suction
To either shore, and he
May not witness this either. Who knows?
Who knows? That lifelong question.

He tries not to prophesy
What constitutes his future,
Quietly urging himself instead
To consider what little he can know,

Or at least can see: for instance,
These tiny, wriggling specks

In the granular stuff under trees:
Snow fleas, harbingers

Of the sugar-maker's season.
Perhaps he'll stay with that,
Will end with sweet figuration
As home rises into sight

THE STROLLER
~ Phillis Levin

Odessa Steps, Eisenstein's *Battleship Potemkin*

And aren't we all like this at times,
Bumping helplessly down the stairs

    Into a street surging with fire,
    The one whose eyes were upon us

Out of control of the handle
Attached to our carriage?

    Why are we shocked when
    The glasses drop and the face

Of horror crowds the screen?
The reel crackles, there is

    No end in sight,
    Nowhere to flee.

We have seen them before,
People who look surprised

    To have lived so long: open
    An album, pass a wooden door.

Late summer, the quiet creatures
Scurrying through grass

    Know it's time to start over,
    Theirs a genesis we cannot reenter.

MINE, YOURS
~ translated by Ani Gjika

A doll, the same height as my six year old self,
same gray-colored eyes, dark hair
with the same fear of the dark and charmed by it,
one of few things my mother would save.
"Do not touch it!" I was told.
"I have nothing else to sell if we go broke!"
Until the day when I secretly stole her
and playing, broke her heel.
It was no longer capital, worth nothing now.
Then it became mine.

The day I met you, it was May,
impeccable, blue with a few white clouds at the edge
and nothing more
like miniature drawings on a cookie box
to whet the appetites of angels, not humans.
What could I do to own such a day
except give it a hard kick in the heel?

For Achilles, the heel would have had no use
if he hadn't had to choose between glory and a happy life.
Happiness is anonymous, a face without features; it belongs to no one.
But glory, yes. Even to this day he drags it behind him,
his one and only divine defect.
Motherland? I doubt such a place even exists,
that between her and me there's any cracked glass,
an ethereal wound, an undeniable physical reality
no matter which side of it bleeds.
We do everything to own life,
"my life", "your life",
when in fact, the opposite happens.

Life needs more than a heel to fasten you to itself,
it hits you hard on the neck
and split in two, with no time for awe
you find yourself one day
exhibited in two separate museums at once.

At this very moment, even I am not sure,
which part is the one speaking to you,
and which is the one the docent's pointer's commenting on.

E Imija, E Jotja
~ original by Luljeta Lleshanaku

Një kukull, që kishte gjatësinë time prej 6 vjeçareje,
ngjyrën e syve të mi gri, flokë të errët
dhe të njejtën frikë dhe joshje nga errësira,
—ishte nga të paktat gjëra që ruante ime më.
"As mos iu afro!" —më ishte thënë.
"Nuk kam se çfarë tjetër të shes nëse mbetemi keq!"
Deri atë ditë që e mora fshehurazi,
dhe në lojë e sipër, i prisha thembrën.
Nuk vlente më për kapital; nuk vlente më për asgjë.
Atëherë u bë e imja.

Dita kur të njoha ty, ishte një ditë maji,
e përkryer, krejt e bardhë, me ca re të vogla blu në cep,
e asgjë tjetër,
si dizajani minimalist në ambalazhin e një kutie biskotash,
për të hapur oreksin e engjëjve, jo njeriut.
Çfarë duhet të bëja për ta bërë timen atë ditë,
përveçse një goditjeje të fortë në thembër?

Kurse Akilit, nuk do t'i bënte punë thembra,
nëse nuk do t'i duhej të zgjidhte midis jetës së lumtur dhe lavdisë.
Lumturia është anonime, një fytyrë pa tipare; nuk i përket askujt.
Kurse lavdia, po. Të cilën e tërheq sot e kësaj dite,
pas defektit të tij të vetëm hyjnor.

Atdheu? Unë do të dyshoja edhe nëse ekziston diçka e tillë,
sikur midis meje dhe tij të mos ishte një xham i krisur,
një plagë eterike, që pavarësisht se në cilën anë pikon,
e bën atë një realitet të pamohueshëm fizik.

Ne bëjme gjithçka për të pasur pronësi mbi jetën,
"jeta ime", "jeta jote"...
kur në të vërtetë ndodh krejt e kundërta.
Asaj nuk i mjafton veç thembra për të të lidhur pas vetes,
por të jep një goditje të fortë në zverk,
dhe i ndarë më dysh, pa pasur as kohë për habi,
një ditë e gjen veten,
të ekspozuar në dy muze të ndryshëm njëkohësisht.

Pikërisht tani, as unë nuk jam e sigurtë,
se cila prej pjesëve, është ajo që po ju flet
se mbi cilën po bën koment shkopi i ciceronit.

THE FIRST LOVE
~ William Logan

Rembrandt, *Saskia with Pearls in Her Hair*, 1634

Waddled might have been the word.
After decades, someone you loved

comes swanning back to your life.
Mostly, it turns out, there are reasons.

Yet there she was, in the lobby of Lincoln Center,
that bell-like voice floating over the crowd.

At sixteen, she had been the smartest girl
in the junior class—raven-haired,

shadow-eyed, with a rough flare of a smile,
and always a slight mockery to her voice.

One day, she came down the stairs
wearing a new ankle-chain, and I knew it was over.

She walked out of the opera-goers,
drowning in scarves, a hundred pounds heavier.

"Have I changed?" In that tiny etching,
double-chinned, Saskia stares vacantly

off the laid paper, pearls done up
in the burin's light scratch of her hair,

a plump young woman wholly conventional,
but to the artist, who saw himself so harshly,

she must have been everything. "Have I changed?"
That voice brought back the life so expensive to regret.

ODE TO PEEP TUBES AND THEIR MAKERS
~ Thomas Lux

Let's say peep tubes
are a pair of lenses ground and polished,
and attached at each end
in a manner which brings forth
the heretofore unseen,
from the so tiny as to be invisible
to the nude eye,
to the so massive but so far no unaided eye could see it either.
To discover the nearer, invisible world! What's that wormy
blur writhing in a drop of water?
In a dollop of sperm—are those tiny animalcules
baby boys or baby girls? The better the peep tubes
the more they saw, some of it not
good: a lesion inside a tumor hiding in the corner
of a single cell. Some of it good: a clue to a poison
which'll close a lesion's trapdoor
and make a tumor swallow itself.
I like, too, the collapsible peep tube the captain snaps
open to read a distant ship's flag. Time
to haul out the powder kegs
or pull alongside for plum cakes and canary wine?
To see things no other eye has seen, I have relied,
since childhood, on peanuts. When I split
these curvy (similar to early fertility symbols) legumes
I am Anton van Leeuwenhoek,
I am Galileo Galilei, I'm a captain on the deck
of a thirsty ship, a hungry ship,
and I see land through my peep tube
freshwater falls, mild humans,
and I turn to my shipmates and say,

however a sailor says it: Heave to, or ho, boys,
this way, over there, I see land!

MUMBLETY PEG
~ Maurice Manning

You don't see people whittling like
you used to. It's like whittling is out,
along with mumblety peg, the kind
of game some boys would play in a barn
some afternoon. People are tired
of the old Americana stuff,
the hokey scenes on calendars,
the beauty of a cat-eye marble. And yet,
if you're a whittler all you need
is time, a pocketknife, and a stick
and you're in business. I had a teacher
who made a dog from a bar of soap,
right there in the classroom in front of us.
We marveled how the shape took shape.
I made a fantastical rooster once
from a stick. His comb was out of proportion
to his little body. He wasn't persuasive
as a rooster, but who expects a rooster
to be persuasive anyway.
And my grandfather carved an elephant
from a peach pit. The skill he had
is evident. But I wonder why
he wanted to use something small
to represent something large?
What was going through his mind
in 1920, whenever it was?
In a drawer somewhere I have the knife.
The handle is made from bone and the blades
are worn down to nubs. I used
to use it when I played mumblety peg.
The old knife is sitting there

in the drawer with some cat-eye marbles
and a couple of dominoes. I used
to like to hear them click together.
It was a very particular click.

AGE
~ Gail Mazur

I'd study an old man in a dune garden, his gnarly feet
planted in a swathe of blue salvia,
pruning a low-growing red rose he called Europeana.

Each summer a new project, dear labor, digging,
replanting, weeding, terracing, taming
the sandy slope—still, always beneath it

the lively indomitable dune. Mornings, afternoons,
dusk, the shrill cries of seagulls.
Moonlight, prehistoric. I watched as if to osmose,

to take in the flame of concentration, as if I'd learn
how it was to be lost myself in a saving task.
But you can't choose who or what claims you.

Though sometimes it seemed he'd live forever—each tier
of seedlings a stanza he'd go on and on
revising—it was only that one century, ten little decades.

Ten decades, ten worlds of change, of fabrication
and horror, ten worlds he never tired of.
The garden's gone, now, the lilies, the anemones, the gardener

a tiny body in a cemetery's fidgeting sand by
the white eroded markers of Yankee sea captains
and Azorean fishermen. I'd always thought there was no

weight to him, no guilt or sorrow, he was an ethereal spirit,
that ambition had finally cast him off,
stranded him, as if he lacked the heft of a neutrino

and was moving faster than the speed of light—
all worldliness subsumed—
but that wasn't really him I'd been studying, not him,

just an idea trying to form itself, an idealization of age,
a bearable fiction a world of tenderness
and nurturing where I'd enjoy my books and papers,

my gardens, where what I'd tend would know to blossom
and each death be followed by renewal.
Those were the days I had almost everything I loved,

Until it happened the world shook, and my life
whispered to me, *Come closer, Gail,
look! I won't hurt you*, and I had to look—and it did.

KAFKA (1924)
~ Campbell McGrath

That people truly are as they appear, wearing hats
in the street, chewing pencils at work,
even naked in bed, in passion—that this is so
continually arouses in me
feelings of the most extreme astonishment.

*

Gravestones are teeth in the jaw
of the devouring earth, are they not?
Precious incisors, holy relics.
Thus we explain the crooked smiles
on the faces of all the angels in the paintings.

*

The way water runs through coffee grounds,
taking on new life, scorched
and exhilarated by the process, the process,

and then the coffee comes into focus,
dark as blood, transformed utterly—

if our lives could aspire to such revision,

if only we could mimic the miraculous
strip of celluloid though which the projector
casts its beam of light and desire
toward the awaiting movie screen.

*

This is no fairy tale.
The man approaching from the shadows is indeed a torturer.

The mouth he seals may be mine, but the wrists
he binds with shackles, the calipers, the subtle blades—

can you not understand
it is your own flesh to be torn?

*

Every draft, every notebook, every word—
burn it all,
Max, burn everything.

POEM
~ Maureen N. McLane

The gabble in the night
you said must be turkeys—

after the babble
of the sweating city

what to make
of the rhodomontade

of the bullfrog?
The peepers

outshriek the club kids.
The metallic

screech of the grate
cranked upward

by the guy at the newsstand—
morning orison

crossed by a single crow.

DIASPORA
~ Erika Meitner

I am riding the F train to Brooklyn with my son, who is Appalachian as
much as anything, who is six and does not notice the Hasidic women
reading Tehilim, praying psalms on the way home from worn leather-
bound siddurim, moving their lips past Broadway, Second Avenue,
Delancey, since he would not know to identify them by their below-
the-knee skirts, the filled in parts on their shaytls where scalp should
be visible, or the Brighton Beach men in grey fedoras and vaguely
menacing hand-tattoos speaking Russian, the sometimes wondrous
mosaic murals or regular green and white tiles spelling station names:
Bergen St., Carroll St., Smith 9th St., my son discovering he can see
his own reflection in the windows of the cars when they plunge into
the dark tunnels while the women's lips keep moving, and I want to tell
him I know their kind, though I know to say this would be reductive
or offensive even if I might say it too about the bleach blond with the
septum ring, or the old Russian mobsters, so when he says, *It's hard to
believe that you got off here every day*, I agree with him and think of all
the times I climbed the station stairs or felt the give of metal turnstiles
on my hips, the jangle of apartment keys or click of my own heels
on pavement after a night out too late the car service guys playing
dominoes on overturned crates outside the bodega who didn't look
up the way the trains vibrated beneath the surface with exactly the
frequency they always did, blowing hot air through the grates, rattling
me to the bone with foreboding joy and I want to tell him I know this
exact moment, the one where you finally learn the contours of your
own face, its beauty as it hurtles through darkness

EPIPHYTES & NEOPHYTES
~ Drew Milne

said lichen finds association
in fungus with photosynthetic
symbionts a stable vegetative
structure that bodes as being
how fungus found discovery in
mutual agriculture as extreme
adversity from isolated rocks
and deserts to a tune of many

in this generalised sense the
said find crusty leafy frondy
squamulose even leprose quite
demeaning in a typical growth
off from human namer projects
the grave mark despite energy
shared in parasitic symbiosis
and all given up to semantics

the taxonomy fictions revised
by each genera of new science
are so efficient in absorbing
all too slow maturation files
into a stressful low resource
research paradigm environment
suited for adaptation to most
funding demands to become art

ultimate pioneer plants being
stark reality the habitat and
colony is a laboratory reason
and a food for reindeer moose

some deer and flying squirrel
even to the snub-nose monkeys
of China and human rock tripe
in search of starvation stuff

famine worlds take from hints
manna from heaven as a desert
lichen served by the wind for
spent dyes perfumes medicines
poisons and litmus a doctrine
of signatures proving colours
and uses truer than plausible
or worse as in laws and facts

the biological monitors clock
to map pollution PCBs and the
radioactive fallout now fills
falls on into fields or wilds
moves from marine to earthier
life in the Proterozoic Eon's
boring billion so called by a
climate in embracing language

IT'S NO FOX
~ Nancy Mitchell

you'd see the drag
trail and nothing
left save a few feathers

be a skunk that sucks
all the blood out
leaves the body

behind to rot—damned
if those hens don't look
like they just lay

down to sleep, unruffled
corn feed and straw
a necklace blood stuck

WHAT WERE FIREFLIES
~ Nancy Mitchell

Five, maybe I was
six, out on the back stoop
about to first star wish

when Queen Anne's
lace in the lot next door
lit up with what I thought

sparks from my dad's butane
torch, him all liquored up,
finally making good

on his threat to *burn
every single weed
into the goddamn ground.*

LOOP #5: THE BARRANCAS
~ Carol Moldaw

Somewhere inside poems written
to avoid unwritable ones
are wisps of what I turned from.
If not inside, then suspended,
like a full moon at 6 a.m., drained
of color in a rust ring of cloud.

I like to time things to the minute
but having 15 minutes leeway
is more reliable, allows for time
spent watching the puff and dissolve
of contrails fat as SUV tracks
in the arroyo's impressionable sand.

To register to scale what's intangible,
I take the ridge to where the trail
tapers off and the view expands,
range after range, our own house,
small from here, one among many,
just past the curve of silver poplars.

METRICS
~ Carol Moldaw

Though the earnestness of artists bores me
as do admonitions in art,

I admit I begrudge certain words
for worming their way into my poems.

Too bad I can't hang up on them,
as on a robo-call or marketing survey.

A word shouldn't diminish the thing it names.
Who would want to "engage in foreplay"?

Fellatio's at least a word worth mouthing.
I also notice I've gotten more attentive, more

painstaking, regarding my likes and dislikes
and less bemused by those of others.

"Does the Dalai Lama fly coach?"
the dowager asks the table, a flirty laugh

underscoring her point: one-up on him
and, though a widow, nobody's fool.

To whom but me do these metrics matter?
To whom but me, this pain, that shame?

DENY THE ROOSTER
~ Glenn Mott

A hundred names in every thousand here is
Wu Ming (无名), pronounced *nameless.*

In Guizhou we were colored men (白人),
pronounced Byron, or *Bái sè de ren.*

Spiritual junkies. We are the cold
whites around the yolk.

To those who don't test me as a *piàn zi,*
a *cheat*, I happily pay the foreign tax.

We are treated well
by those who don't use us as ATMs.

But give what gifts you have.
Sometimes the 白人 will be

grateful for conversation.
And that will be worth a higher

price for simple dishes, of salt
and oil, peanuts and cucumbers.

NAPALM NOTES
~ Hoa Nguyen

Developed in secret
at Harvard   produced

by Dow Chemical
An efficient incendiary formula

perfected on Valentines Day
1942   A thickened

gasoline   Can be
dropped from planes

(napalm bombs)
also flamethrowers

8 million tons of bombs
in Vietnam   Burns at

1,500–2,200°F (⅕th as hot
as the surface of the sun)

Very sticky   stable
        relatively cheap

THE DOG STAR
~ D. Nurkse

She says: Sirius is rising on our monitors,
so bright the pixels sear our fingertips.
It will cauterize our pupils.
But the actual skies are empty.
If anything a few minor stars,
Koab, Vega, Lyra, are missing.

No bats, no birds, no fireflies.

It peaks in daylight, on any screen,
I-Phone, laptop, EKG display,
Zenith Console cracked in a dumpster,
Nook, I-Pad, Kindle, Cineplex.

They say our names are written forever
in blood-ink in the Book of Life.

But Sirius is pulsing in its own sky.

2
I want to tell her *can't wait* but instead
I begin barking, excitable Pekinese
with a collar of tinkling bells,
a dog with crazy rolling eyes
who doesn't know if his tail is working
in love or anger——a pet infuriated
by his own yapping, to the point
he can't stop, can't stop, can't stop--

She offers a biscuit but holds it
at arm's length. I study that remove
and feel my voice drop, temper,
return to a human prevarication.

Five hundred billion tons of methane welling up
from sinkholes in the permafrost,
flood stage inching above the sea-walls:
too much for words, let alone a sobbing growl.

3
August. I see her face in every mirror,
Isis following Osiris to the shadow world.
She stares back, about to speak,
but between our lips a cloud forms.

Lick it clean with your red tongue.

OLD MEN IN LOVE
~ D. Nurkse

Old men with protruding abdomens like ants;
fixed smiles like dogs; who apologize
for the sweetish smell of mucilage;
who corral you in their tenements
to show you their stamp collections—

what a strange country of forking rivers,
waterfalls, adamant cliffs, young girls
strolling with parasols, as if there were paths,
and so *miniature*: old men who breathe

on the thick lens and wipe it
to bring out a detail—a peach tree,
a thatched cottage, in its gated window
an unlit lamp—and in each narrow sky

there is a faint cancelled number.

THE SEASONS OF THE DAY
~ William Olsen

—Thoreau

We know too much about ourselves,
and we have talked creation half to death,
but I cherish going on in words.

A green leaf contained a gold leaf.
This is the one and only season of
this one and only waking hour and even when I listen,

even when I shut up I'm still shrill.
Dawn almost ceases to live and begins to be
the smallest of birds.

What season shall we name this distant waking hour?
What would be called spring when it's October all day,
and November would do us in?

A few hours into the done-and-gone a low-down
disgusted wind that doesn't know why it's windy
dies down to an awareness of awareness.

Creepy. And the lake has nothing to say.
This season of cynical cresting smiles.
Another hour, another, ending in reflection if I'm standing

high enough on a bluff and above it all
taking in the panoramic dead-reckoned
desolate waves that are always in season.

What season of the day did I feel no self-pity,
never begrudged friends their loveliness,
never slandered a single person

out loud or in my angelic heart,
and never despised my beloved
for being gentler than I will be,

It is not my weakness before others I despise,
not hatred that hangs me out to dry.
Quiet village avenues, I listen in, too.

I can almost hear the light falling asleep.
Tree shade shallows to twilight
and a deer not fawn but not yet a yearling looks up.

The look of this deer says with perfect mercy
get your own twilight and invisibility,
be busy right now with your own story.

I'm sitting in a booth of a place called Friendly's.
Old friend I haven't seen in decades.
We have seen our own way to seating ourselves.

I find myself in the company of words.
My friend ending an astonishing story
is suddenly stricken, ashamed by his own enthusiasm.

In the last season of the day he finishes the story, it's real.
A guy in a lifeboat catches a seagull that lands on his head
after an eternity lost in the Pacific.

I'm eating my literal fries.
I have no idea who this person really is any more.
This is the season of memory and leavetaking and

he looks old when his voice says old and old says
It'd be a wonder if I made it to 85.
Yeah and then you look around and really wonder.

130 seconds or 130 years of consciousness—
it's a miracle that we are even talking.
One day we won't know which of us said what.

Now one of us is going on about some new theory
about the universe being finite
because infinity, a limited concept,

is only human.

FACK YOU
~ Dzvinia Orlowsky

Father called us into our room, sat on the edge of one twin bed, head lowered, then lifting up his eyes asked: *Have either of you ever heard of the word … "fack"*? He pronounced it like he pronounced *"mashrooms,"*— immigrant doctor ordering pizza at Fatbob's when Mother came up short on chicken livers or tripe. He looked at us in disbelief, his now foul-mouthed daughters. A houseguest had overheard us—me— scream *fuck!* while driving the ping-pong ball directly into the net, my sister spinning wildly on her heels, her *ha-ha's* booming up from the dusky basement paneled with faux brick, a half-case of 16-ounce cokes already chugged between us. We ached to be *Greaser* girls of teased hive hair, the runs in their black nylons an arrow to their jutting hips as they slouched against the dumpster smoking Lucky Strikes behind the pizza joint, a secret society of popularity and sin waiting for Greaser boys to slink through, slicked hair and black Banlon shirts, flipping the finger to anyone who dared even walk past them—*Go Fuck yourselves you Fuckin' Mother Fucker!*—Instead we were Father's two angels carrying pails of water to a thirsty horse in our desiccated meadow, no shade in sight—and Father, always running late, making his rounds, dressed, always, in his Steve McQueen sky-blue suit, revving his silver roadster T-Bird, a Hell's Angel patient coming in for an allergy shot, catching him instead napping on the gynecologist's table, his feet up in the stirrups, an open can of Seven-up next to him. America had opened its arms. But he had not done his job. At day's end, in the parking lot surrounded by poppers pinging in shallow marshes, in a moment of freedom, we knew, forgiven, he'd put the blame on the *pleased-with-herself* house guest warming herself like a fat August fly at our front window. *Fack her*, he'd whisper, fumbling for his keys.

A. IN SEPTEMBER
~ Kathleen Ossip

A piece of you flew into me one day, a
Niggling hooked little finger of spirit. I was
Driving. It didn't hurt, it tickled.
Randomly, I'd been thinking I'd become a baby cuddler.
Even though I didn't have a baby anymore, I could substitute.
After all, lots of hospitals must need cuddlers.

Forget it, I thought immediately. It wouldn't be the same.
Oh! It tickled when I knew it would never be the same and I
Remembered suggesting it to you once, when you were
Sad there were no more babies in your life, no
Toddlers, your grandchildren were tweens now—
Except you didn't like the idea. You wanted a connection you couldn't
Really get from a scheduled cuddle with an unrelated baby,

Only from an impossible baby of your own.
So you had limitations too. What you taught me:
Screw limitations. Love anyway, and hard.
I remembered this when it flew, the
Piece in me of you.

BANGLADESH
~ Alicia Ostriker

It is where the driver was born
and still has family,
eighteen people to support.
I have thanked him for the Bollywood music
on his radio, and he sighs, a long elegiac sigh,
like a man who secretly knows how soon
the world will be under water
but does not wish to discuss it.

Everything is in the hands of the Gods.
Nonetheless he wishes to speak,
to explain his life to me, to say
In fifteen years he has had only one accident,
which was not at all his fault
but the police always think the taxi driver
is the guilty one.
It cost him four thousand dollars.
Now he is more cautious about everything,
like a turtle, he says, turning his head sharply.

In Bangladesh they drive even worse.
The death rate is terrible, but what are you going
to do? He gets out to open my door,
a courtesy unasked. His bald dome shines like brass
in the May sunset that tenderly strokes it
reaching across the river
its cashless compensation
while he manages a complex mix
of bowing, smiling, and sighing
all at the same time.

I mirror his motion, the two of us
acting like long-estranged kin
awkward, awkward ,
and cautious.

RENUNCIATION
~ Linda Pastan

Like flowers
with knife-sharp
petals—

scions
of the sunflower
family—

the bright arrows
of beauty are aimed
at the heart.

So pain hides
in the billowy garments
of pleasure,

wounding
the open eye,
the listening ear.

An end, please, to all
sensation. Close
the museums,

lock the keys of the pianos
in their long, dark
coffins.

I choose an unlit room
and medicinal
sleep. I summon

for company,
dim and silent as fog,
only my old ghosts.

HOW TO SAY THANK YOU IN FRENCH
~ Molly Peacock

http://www.wikihow.com/Say-Thank-You-in-French

Method 1: *Basic Thanks*

1
Say "merci." This is the standard, most basic way of saying "thank you" or "thanks" in French.

Merci for seeing me.
To be seen, important thing in life, most.

2
Add "madame" or "monsieur" after it. If you want your merci to sound a little more formal, you could address the other person as "madame" or "monsieur" after expressing your gratitude.

Merci, madame for not raising your eyebrows at *mon monsieur,*
spécialement when I declare,
"I think I'm going to get married again."

Method 2: *Adding Emphasis*

1
Use "merci beaucoup." This phrase means "thank you very much" or "many thanks."

Merci beaucoup for asking to meet him.
Merci beaucoup for saying, "I've always liked men with his looks."
Merci beaucoup for your silence as I hysterically mention that *mon fiancé* has just passed the five-year cancer recurrence mark.

Silence.

2

Switch to "merci bien." This is another expression used to say "thank you very much." *Bien* is usually used to mean "well" or "good," but it can also mean "very" ... *bien* is being used to express emphasis on the strong nature of the thanks.

Merci bien for twenty-one years of taking his side as I railed against his habits: setting the alarm, all timed to his shockingly limited point of view. (Everything isn't always logic you know!)

Merci bien for *vingt et un* years of a quiet standing beside a sliver of a shadow of his logique while never saying I am *une névrosée. Hysterique.* Usually about *rien.*

3

Express extreme gratitude with "mille fois merci." This expression roughly translates into "a thousand times thanks" or "thanks a thousand times."

Mille fois merci for your voice: a rich, calm sea. As if a person heard the sea from lying on the beach in a painting by Matisse: *Luxe, Calme et Volupté.*

Là, tout n'est qu'ordre et beauté, Baudelaire a écrit. There, all is order and beauty. Henri et Charles were right, you were right. Why get *nerveux* about it all? How about a little more *volupté,* or *calme,* at least?

To be heard, important thing in life, most.

Method 3: *Full Sentence Format*

1

Tell someone familiar "Je te remercie." This translates to "I thank you." ... *Te* is a second person pronoun used to indicate that you are speaking to someone you are familiar with. It can be used with friends and family.

Je te remercie for your painterly point of view.
Did you always have to paint me a picture?
Yes, to learn anything, I had to see it.

It was as if I gave you all the elements and you reassembled them into a 45-minute painting—who am I kidding? I mean 90 minutes since I never got anything done in a single session.

Je te remercie, je te remercie for the *petite* capacity inside me for stepping outside myself. Yes! *C'est possible!* How little my mother could step outside. But she tried valiantly. What a deep love had we. *Ma mère limitée. Je te remercie* for the sea, *la mer*, in your voice.

2
Switch to "C'est vraiment gentil de ta part." This expression means, "It is really kind of you."

C'est vraiment gentil de ta part to be really kind to me. To remember that your kindness leads my kindness since I was born into violence.

C'est vraiment gentil de ta part to remind me, that yes, each of us is many-roomed.

In my mansion, in a drawer in a cabinet upstairs in a locked room lies a painted ivory miniature, its perspective from the bottom of a flight of stairs. My sister, *ma sœur*, and *moi*, look from the last step up to the top, into the face of:

Le Monstre!

Le Monstre Papa,
face red from *alcool,*
pushes a woman down the stairwell.
Our *Maman.*

Others have guest rooms, not intruder *chambres*. From others I have learned kindness. And French. *C'est vraiment gentil de leur part.*

It's very kind of them. Kindness is wealth. And words. It was very kind of you, *mon analyste.*

3
Tell someone you do not know well "Je vous remercie." This is a more formal, less familiar way to say, "I thank you." ... *Vous* is a more polite way to address someone in the second person "you," so this phrase is generally used with strangers and elders. For further emphasis, you could also say "*Je vous remercie de tout cœur*," meaning, "I thank you from the bottom of my heart."

Now that you have become stranger and elder after your terrible stroke, I use *vous*. Formal, no?

You speak a strange language, mixing up pronouns and sending your doorman's neck snapping back to look at us when you address him as SHE.

Je vous remercie de tout coeur for being alive. To have you return from the dead allows me to thank you from the bottom of my heart, which long ago I attempted to freeze in imitation of *ma mère*, who froze her heart against *le monstre.*

But my attempt freeze-dried my heart instead!
When *ma soeur*, whom he violated,
came in desperation with a knife to hack my heart out,
it had dried into bits.
You and I have pieced the flinty fragments together.
Je vous remercie, je vous remercie de tout coeur.

4
Express formal written thanks with "Je vous adresse mes plus vifs remerciements." This expression is often included in formal letters and means, "I send you my most sincere thanks" or "I send you my warmest thanks."

Now that you repeat the same words over and over, I cannot talk too regularly on the telephone with you. For something sears into me after we have the same conversation *encore et encore*. I hang up the phone and sit listless in the country where I voyaged to marry my logical individual, still very much alive.

But I express my formal thanks, *plus vifs*, in cards, pictures of the sea, which you will never cross again. For after several years of saying, "If I could only get to Europe again," you changed the words, "I know I won't get there any more."

Are you sad? *Triste?*

"A little," *un petit peu*, "but I am at peace with it."

Une paix personnelle. How *volupté*, to imagine you checking the bank of metal mail boxes in your New York City building, there finding a square envelope of *luxe* paper sent from Toronto. Inside: a picture of *la mer*, where all is order and beauty! Open *la carte* to these words, *Je vous adresse mes plus vifs remerciements.* For my second chance, *merci.* Later you will call and repeat, "How lucky I am." *J'ai de la chance*, you say. And I say, *J'ai de la chance* back to you.

NEW MOON HAFTORAH
(*ISAIAH* 66: 1–24)
~ Robert Pinsky

I hate your new moons, your appointed holidays,
God says. A boy pipes the memorized syllables,
Koh aumar! Adonai, hashawmayim keesee.

God hates your empty rituals and sacrifices.
He says it's like watching you cut a dog's throat
Machey-eesh ohveyach hazeh aureyf keleb.

In the clear high-pitched voice earnestly chanting
Uncomprehending the mighty sounds, God says:
Behold, the faithful city has become a whore.

By fire and by the sword will the Lord deal
With all who sanctify themselves and hide in
Gardens to eat the flesh of swine and of mice.

Mere gestures of worship disgust the Lord. The child
Faitihfully sings the disintegrating words,
Losheh kay-awkh, like one whom his mother comforteth.

In the child's fresh voice the old melody promises
He will make, between one new moon and another,
Ahil ehrkhat: new heavens and a new earth.

WALL CALENDAR
~ Lia Purpura

That's one day
fewer
you get to have.
One you had
and lived
that's gone.
Crossed out.
You get more,
but dosed
and measured
(though with
one line
you can make
a day into
two triangles,
a week of sailboats,
or a month
of good, hard
sideways rain.)

TRADITION
~ Lia Purpura

Someone soon
will be gored by a bull
as happened last summer,
and will again
in summers to come.
A bull goes off course,
a man trips
as he runs—
circumstances change,
but the bull
is slaughtered
in the end.
The event could be
quit altogether,
or altered,
made kinder,
but then time
or something
wouldn't work right.
The ripening of fruit or
the reddening leaves
aren't enough
to alert anyone
to death in the town,
on the street,
there would be
no whisper
around every corner
come closer, I'm here,
death saying

*you want
to touch me,
that's it, isn't it?*

A COUPLE OF DISASTERS AND A LOT OF LANDSCAPE
~ Lawrence Raab

for Carin Clevidence

First the explosion of the fireworks factory,
later the hurricane. First a tree full
of tiny American flags, then no trees at all.

A long story needs at least one disaster
to show us how people act when they're caught
off guard, whereas the landscape
in between is a good place for detail

and second thoughts. *Yes,* she decides,
that's why I never answered his letter,
or went out that night in the rain.
The writer knows the trick is always
balance. Too much thinking is worse

than too much action, except for Proust.
And many other equally persuasive exceptions,
which remind us the best advice exists
to be disregarded once it's understood.

Aftermath is for the difficult truths.
Is that where our house used to be?
the wife asks, hoping the answer isn't
what she can see so clearly—
many pages torn from a book, and a spoon,

the umbrella no one ever used, two letters
still unopened—all the secrets of debris,
and everything they mean if they mean
anything beyond the strangeness of what survives.

WHAT LIGHT TASTES LIKE
~ Barbara Ras

Depends on the hour of departure and if flowers
or fruits, maybe the lacy grapeyness of kudzu in early fall,
for all its artsiness a killjoy at heart. I will rot
before I regret being driven from Gaylord Drive,
though I'll miss the calls from the first floor to announce—bluebirds,
red-tailed hawk, their ballooning in warm light that tasted oddly like ice.

To enter certain caves you must first
disinfect your feet to avoid contaminating the animals
painted on stone, often with their own blood and lost ingredients.
If I tried I could find the breathless bat I brought home from Italy
after sitting on its inconspicuous flatness in a gazebo overlooking a lake,
a shiny lake, where days earlier we'd kayaked with Michele
in light that tasted like the lips of a prophet who whispered
"Trust the glaze on the water," his lips one pink up
from transparent.

Sometimes I suspect suspicion has the foretaste of death, a state
as starless as it gets, and once on a hunch
I searched the obits online to learn a friend—
not close, but dear—had gone.
The light of knowing was nothing like the light shining
from her crystalline poems and from her half-wolf dog,
who put his paws on my chest to stand above me
and bow his creamy head
to look down at me with longing.
His aquamarine gaze stole light
from the north, and I now see Vera and her dog, whose name
I've forgotten but whom I'll call Olaf, riding a train, a long journey
to Siberia, Baikal, deepest of all lakes on earth,

making it the most seeingest of eyes, full of light
that tastes like the bread of the people here who cook with sour milk
and mimic bird calls and clucks.

Let Vera and Olaf spend all their days now, working with
water, water that has seen an incalculable number
of stars—Olaf lighting paths in the dark with his blue eyes and Vera
laughing her flinty laugh praising the sky and its clouds—while they
    kneel
to take half an infinity's worth of lake to distill all the starlight it has held,
purifying it for endless time until it tastes like our first elements,
until it tastes like us.

LOOKING ACROSS THE LINE
~ Alberto Ríos

Looking from the American to the Mexican side, there
The colors come from far south, or from bougainvillea

Itself, these colors from sky and parrot and bananas.
The turquoise is from dreams, where it was invented.

But more curious are all the small houses themselves
Glued precariously onto the hills just across the line,

So many, crowded in a bouquet of odd geometries.
The houses are so close because there are no streets.

Take note: To get to these houses, one must walk.
There are trails, but no roads. It takes a while to notice.

Looking over at the American side from Mexico,
Streets and cars are everywhere and go everywhere—

There are more businesses than houses, more everything,
More granite walls than worn trails, more trees,

More signs than windows, more grocery stores.
And, quietly, nondescript, there are government offices.

They're big, but they don't make a noise, these animals,
Content to crouch ominous as tigers, waiting.

They do not show their colors. They hide very well
Their orange and black, until it is too late for you.

I CAN'T SPEAK SO
~ David Rivard

I can't speak so easily of why all's noise
that bothers me recently because can't
hear myself think that well amid the sawing
and hammering of non-union carpenters,
never mind the drunk singing of backyard
neighbors, who after all just want to
live a little & not interrogate themselves
as to the soul & its arrangements (which are
mostly secret—the soul coming & going
like a message banded to a pigeon's leg,
and just as light), but perhaps my mother's
quietness got to me as a child & so
I crave now more of same I associate
with her either loving or anxious
in preoccupied pacing in the sun parlor
or park playground her feelings & thoughts
as they crossed the airspace a tone
unspoken but there to catch, a spell, her signal
subtle but clear—the brain is an antenna
for the mind, the French say (or so Sarah
Stickney tells me), & maybe by being so
can pick up on what's inaudible to ears
but clear even amid the shouting that
surrounded one once as a child sliding gleefully
on fresh sawdust the apprentice butchers
had scattered over varnished oak planking
in the President Avenue meat market—my
mother's look that day somewhere in silence
a question I still can't answer—"why are you
doing that?"—*why?*—*I dunno*— why do I
even need to know?—not a single answer

in my head really—just a vibration—the vexed
but coppery-bright buzz that likewise
comes if you cup a loud cricket in your hand.

SOLASTALGIA
~ Clare Rossini

Dressed in Sunday best,
My brothers lean together atop the backyard hill:

Ray with his wise-guy grin, the tie pinching his neck,
Tony in sailor suit, nursing his thumb—

What bird coursing overhead
Has stolen his glance away from some adult's *Smile, say cheese*—?

Beyond the figures, a landscape
Trapped in the snapshot's range of tender grays,

Just enough
Shadow and light to suggest

That airy, indeterminate space   duck-traversed, grass-hoppered
Its paths as random as the uninscribed   trails of wind.

And in winter, the sand pile   a rounding frozen
Until March loosened   ice skins breaking, mottled browns

Morphing to a green   too tremendous to be held by the eye.
The earth of that place   opening

Not like a book   not even like a hymn
The bells of the church down the street   breaking their bronzed lament

New bungalows rising to the west   ancient oak scattered among them
Their arms still   opening to sky....

It had no name, that place. Even now, I call it *field,* and still
It slips the tether.

*

Pascal, provincial who skirted the salons with the wistfulness
Of one who leaned toward infinites, unities, magic squares

Nonetheless had the chutzpah to thumb his nose at Aristotle
And rattle his elder, Descartes

When he proved by experiment (tubes, mercury, a measuring stick)
That nature was indeed rife with vacuums.

And from vacuums, the principals of hydraulics; from hydraulics
    Pascal's dream:

A new machine that will multiply forces to any amount desired
    [Thereby allowing]

A man ... to lift any weight
    That another may propose.

So Thought flits down neural paths and constellates equations
    Wending its way toward the zeal of *Thing*—

    *

As in the bulldozer that appeared   cabled to its flatbed   one hot July noon
    Yellow-bright, oiled.

From the crotch of an oak, I watched   it trundle down its ramp
    Its lifted blade skimming

The epiphanic   tips of the reeds.
    The worms far below   stunned in their cool tunnels.

But no alarm, no outcry—
    We needed more walls and roofs   doors, decks, barbeques

And the field, after all, of no note   no mythic cliffs, no rocks
    Moved by paracletes

All its shrines were minor.
    From the heights   I could see the man-shape in the cab—

Sunlight strobing across his hands   as they worked the levers.
    The milkweed patch

The first to go, there   where caterpillars had groined their crypts
    To stiff green stems—

(Each morning, I'd lower my ear   to a chrysalis, hoping to catch
    The sound of worm

Dissolving into the mash   from which flight
                         Arouses itself....)

*

There are those among us who would rather die than cut down a tree.
Not me, says my friend, lifting his finger

To get the waiter's attention. *Perfect,*
He says as the waiter pours.

Give me light bulbs, anesthesia,
I add. *Ships bringing us* (I lift my glass) *merlot—*

To merlot!
We clink, when rain beating on the restaurant's sheathing

Of paned glass
Suddenly quiets the room, candles flickering as, head by head, we turn

To take in the sudden
Savage downpour. *Remember*

The painting we saw this afternoon—? my friend asks. I turn back
To him, nodding. *Thomas Cole—*

Hill overlapping hill, slowly drawing the eye toward the background's
Perspective-perfect mountain, distant summit topped

With a tiny splotch of red—human fire—
The vanishing point.

*

These, my lost,
Tetherless dears:

Ray at 53, dead of a freak infection. Tony, his neural paths silting in,
Wandering the midnights of a group home

Looking for hands to hold,
Faces to touch.

But the field's black-eyed susans, their centers shading toward
The flashpoint of petals—

What theology posts them to a loamy heaven? And who requiems
The bristle-weed,

That kvetch of razored leaf that nonetheless cranked out
Purple blooms?

Late in life, migraines rattling his head, fist of cancer
Tightening in his gut, Pascal—

"That soul permanently ill at ease"—saw a vast darkness opening
From the side of his chair.

Staggered across the room, sat again. *Dear God!* Again loomed
The void, alive

Even in the most ordinary of things.
And so Pascal came to know

The God of Geometry "insufficient"; declared the worship of fact,
And fact alone, would lead to "obscurity and darkness";

The heart has its reasons
That reason cannot know.

In the snapshot's background, a faint shadow, ragged and tall:
The beech, the field's only tree.

I lay beneath it at dusk, the first stars erased and reappearing
Among shifting leaves.

A syllable floated overhead. *Was that*
My name? I rose in the safety of darkness

To see the house on the distant hill, a male shape outlined against
The kitchen door's bright: my father

Calling me home. *No*
I said to the beech. Lying back down in the reeds, I pressed my back

To the damp
Until I was sure I felt

The planet's slow unconscious turn toward freshets of night air.
And then I was the turning.

NONE OF THE ABOVE
~ Mary Ruefle

There are people you love

you never want to see again

and things you love you want to keep

at bay, but it is hardly possible as

they exist so far and so deep inside

yourself, so deep, so deep, how deep,

and everything else exists so far and wide

outside, you spend all your time going

back and forth, if you know what I mean,

it's exhausting, still you must bend with respect

before this revolutionary agent,

even if you never want to see Him again,

He meant that. Sometimes you lie next to someone

nothing else matters, next morning

you wake everything matters, just

lying there thinking about the laundry

then the Telegraph Boy comes

BEGIN AGAIN STOP REVOLUTIONARY AGENT

it's hard, keep trying, come in,

from day to day think of nothing else,

hello, except that it is possible,

it has to be, and anyway otherwise

think of all the things you hate

you could talk about forever.

DEATHBED CONFESSION
~ Ira Sadoff

I don't regret the sailboat I never got when I was ten. Maybe I might have made a great psychiatrist. Holed up in Tuscany instead of Schenectady. Even mastered the clarinet.

But my only lament is that I was less than joyful. I could have used more bliss.

You know how many years I walked in circles holding up a sign? This war, that war, this Dow, that Wal-Mart? Pfizer, you're next! I spent a year in Fredericksburg weeping over graves. Those gardenias by Billie Holiday's headstone, they're mine. There are sharks that sing to me of their extinction.

I hum Perdido after all my stressful love affairs. Now you might not like the music I like, the music I make: it might sound like pots and pans banged together, a technique perfected by grandma Eva of Bialystok to bring us home from danger. She understood, with her chorus of oy-veys, just how wrong everything could be. She was a friend to the helpless, feckless, the miserable bastard I could be, readying me for every allergy, every bee sting, future nights in my self-made monastery.

I don't want to say we're pulled along by some donkey with a plow, I don't want to cash in my bonds to buy a pontoon and putt-putt through lagoons on Sunday afternoons. I want a good Côtes du Rhône, nothing fancy, a little Bird, a smelly cheese, a few strokes from my beloved if there's one in the room. The laugh track from one of Buster Keaton's silent films.

AT THE METROPOLITAN:
EL GRECO'S *VISION OF SAINT JOHN*
~ Grace Schulman

Dazed by the saint's robes, ice-blue, bleached by light,
his arms upraised as though rehearsing a chorus
of dead martyrs, I see unrest: saints' bodies
are moon-white, naked, writhing, as they lunge

for white robes they might wear to the highest throne.
And I wonder why, gazing at warm silks
they've cast aside, colors of sunflowers,
roses, and leaves in spring's first bloom.

Still, they want white. This heaven threatens,
broken, unyielding. Cherubs plummet
as I gasp, hoping their mothy wings will hold.
El Greco's fire-forced painting is unfinished,

just like the souls straining for ascendence.
Torn canvas. A fragment, meant for an altarpiece.
Seeing it now, my mind longs for completeness,
and paints the Lamb to go with Saint John's vision,

not there before, and yet its absence glows.
Now at the gallery, I step aside
for a wheelchair: a young woman, her eyes arcing
to greens, flame-reds, and yellows in the painting,

fragment though it is, and lifts her arms
to the dead, and all I see are hands,
hers, hands of the artist, hands of souls
extended, reaching across four centuries

touching like a sycamore's rangy branches
across a road. I praise the holy unwhole,
the partial, the uneasily unended.
Bless the delay, the wait. Perfection

is never the end-all, not even in heaven.

DOUBLE EFFECT: MARCH 19
~ Martha Serpas

> *Aquinas's Doctrine of Double Effect explains the lawfulness of taking*
> *an action (such as bodily self-defense) that will secondarily cause*
> *serious harm (such as the death of a human being) if the intent of the*
> *action is good and the evil, even if foreseen, is unavoidable.*

It's like this ...

Overall, it has to be a good thing.

Imagine a St. Joseph altar:
St. Joseph and the Christ child
centered before a fan of palms.
Red-white-and-blue bunting overhead—

for some reason—

and your grandmother's pietá
that someone held on her lap for ten hours
from Rome to JFK. Crucifixes,
a Sacred Heart, and more bread,
okra, vegetables of all kinds.

A green bowler cocked on a gold-leafed
photo of a beloved Irish priest.

His face is bigger than Joseph's.
Is *that* the double effect,
blaspheming with the clerical dead?

In the picture the *prie-dieu* is vacant
as a bar after closing. Is this the hubris,
not to give constant thanks?

Any evil here couldn't be like
taking a life to save your own
or giving that last dose of morphine
that you know will salve the pain
but close the door.

Surely it's a great good
to remember a miracle?

You'd also have to foresee an evil ...

what could that be?
Sufficient unto the day

that no one will eat the bread
shaped like sandals? The bread
will go to waste with the poor?
Surely someone will eat
the stuffed artichokes
and all the redfish and catfish and crabs.
What could be wrong with that?

Maybe
          it's that you only have the picture,
and your people, the ones you miss like a drought,
aren't even in the frame
so when they attach it to an email
 and send it to you that very day,

they mean they love you—the greatest good—
but they only break your heart.

GHOST OF THE OLD ARCADE
~ Alan Shapiro

Under the giant chandeliers, in the sunless dazzle,
the objects of desire traded places with desire,

so that to stand there in the middle of that marble
avenue between the plate glass windows

of the shops was to be looked at by our own reflections,
looked at and imagined by them, as if our bodies,

the very matter of us, had been hallucinations all along,
airy specters of a gawking we had to see through

to see what it was we saw. We were always in the way
of what we wanted. Beyond the windows there was only

other windows, smaller windows, reflecting smaller versions
of our faces looking back at us as through the wrong

end of a telescope, adrift on glass vitrines, on the
jeweled surfaces inside them that we couldn't touch:

the diamond facets of a pin, or falling fixed
inside a frozen waterfall of rings and necklaces.

There was glass ware too and cookware, glossy
leather bags and cases all backlit and glittering

as if forged of light by light that promised nothing
but perpetual brightening. And so

to pull away at last from the magnetic
weightlessness of all that show room dreaming;

to tear ourselves from the untouched,
unsullied, the before we had it

having of it, was to trade reflection
for reflection, to see inside the giant prism

of that hall how with our bags and parcels
the body's shadow—shapeless as a sponge—

wiped clean all traces of us from the marble floor
that shone a little brighter for our having gone.

FROM *MAKE YOURSELF HAPPY*
~ Eleni Sikelianos

who did the blue school
who bruised the wound
who had the goddess of love in her lap
to make herself happy—make
a village of love for your shadow
to live in so that
your shadow and your shadow's friends may be
unlonely living with all other ombres
I'm giving away all my belongings
in language   to make myself happy   must start
with "my language"   then find
chains of correspondence
for the world's every articulate hand and finger
(it's what touches the world)
a shadow *hombre* shows me the way toward the deepest umbers
like having an orgasm in your
happy

MY BELLE EPOCH
~ Jeffrey Skinner

I shall fire my image groomer

Hire instead a regular horse

Horse shall tell me Hair ok, shirt ok,

Breath & zipper ok

I shall not engage a groomer

For the horse, horse

Can self-groom

Or, why am I paying?

We shall ride down

The mountain into town,

Me on he, he

In my head, & the villagers

Torches & pitchforks

Surround us—

O, evening cools

The mind turned back

& I beg pardon—

My poems were clearer then

In my belle epoch

THE FAMILY PLOT
~ Floyd Skloot

Through shadows I can see my brother
sink down on his knees, lost in prayer.
Even as it happens I know it could never
happen. Then he is holding the sphinx pose,
doing yoga to welcome solstice. So now
I realize my brother can only be me,
half my age and halfway through a set
of diamond pushups, each one slow
enough to seem like stillness from this
distance. We are in front of an old oak
and the hedge lurking beside us turns
into our parents, angry voices caught
within the hissing wind. Before us all
tombstones tilt in the rain-softened earth.

CHRISTMAS SPECIAL: STANZAS ON ALZHEIMER'S
~ John Skoyles

my mother (1919–2014)

We sat on the couch
drinking tea and watching
Bing Crosby vouch

that Christ is King
while children pushed trucks
around our feet in rings.

She lifted my son,
kissed his chin,
and over music from accordions

said, *John,*
is Santa Claus for real?
Stunned by the question,

my wife gave her the task
of stringing popcorn to a thread
to keep her from asking

anything else, afraid the kids
might doubt
St. Nick's stout slide

down our chimney. I joked
that Santa put on a few pounds
this year, and then she spoke

about Christmastime
as it used to be,
when elves in lines

stocked shelves behind Saks' window
and jolly men on every block
rang bells while yelling *Ho Ho Ho!*

Ho Ho Ho! she repeated,
flushed and proud
as if outfitted

in red and fluffy white—
three syllables
without foresight or hindsight.

A Vigil
~ Ron Slate

Soon it was my turn to sit with the body.

They took away my navel orange and bottle of water,
since to chew and swallow, acts now impossible for the body,
would mock when respect is most required.

My cousins the lawyers were sorting through things
in his apartment—where's the will, the accounts,
the insurance policy? He lived alone there
for twenty-five years, his mother's wig in a drawer,
her dress on a doorhook, his father's clothes in the closet.

He maintained the fiction of being
a business consultant in order to attend trade shows—
technology, textiles, furniture, toys and candy.

During the vigil, it is forbidden to fulfill a commandment,
again, to avoid insulting the limited range of the dead.

But I was remembering, surely a transgression.

His place was stacked high with boxes of brochures,
you could smell the mildewing paper and the demise
of aging materials comprising the house.

At family events he warned us
of the rise of masses of people with grievances—
those who neither invent nor design nor build anything,
those who bloat from food stamps spent on corn chips,
those with no sense of history or culture.

You distribute the wealth, he said, you end with Stalin.

Boxes of free samples, many items no longer for sale—
dried-up ballpoints, baby foods, shoe polish.

By the weeping in the back rows of the chapel,
we were baffled to learn he practiced his dentistry
two days a week in a community clinic.

My cousins found his checkbook and tax returns,
his charity and modest assets. He owed little.
There were no unstamped pages in his passport.

He would talk at length to the disinterested or habitually polite
about Chinese super-high-speed non-shuttle fabric looms.
The surpassing marvels, and then, the cupidity of politicians.

Staring at the ceiling above the body, I could hear
the growing din of drive-time traffic through the walls.

My thirst, my grumbling gut. How many years ago
did I turn my face away from him? He wore a jacket and tie to dinner
but he was not so clean and kempt, as his living space proved.

If there's a man, there's a problem, said Stalin.
No man, no problem.

~ Bruce Smith

I listened with my ear against a glass against a wall. I heard the plans
to gerrymander the body and the mind, to send the children back
where they belong. OK, OK, OK, I heard. Someone's skill is someone's
deviance. Those kids with their ears and busted lips, their hair and
tantrums and counterplans. I covered for them by babbling and crying.

~ Bruce Smith

The suspicion, the fashion, the second guess, the dubious, the bio truth,
the truth that strays, the truth versus improved, distracted truth. Can we
trust the disciples? Can we trust trust? 5 minutes later you're disrupted
by language, you're your vandal, your masseuse. You wanted to become less
baroque and boastful, less provocative. You wanted less excess, excessively.

~ Bruce Smith

So what? was the question after the few wars and marriages
and daughters chased by one mother and undressed by another
[and corn rows braided and un, furrowed and un] and why
are the people like animals they are in tooth and territory
when the animals aren't like that except the swans, gibbons, wolves.

CASH FLOW
~ Charlie Smith

Since you asked, yes,
the hotel is still down the street and the persistence
in capsule form of illusion pertaining to one's standing
in the order of development is, not astounding
exactly, but fraught with the scent of scholarship
and devilment, a casual glance
in itself enough to place you inside the scout hut
at the time of the murder, the joshing
and rib tickling shenanigans of those confined
by the govt for inexplicable acts always out there
just ahead of the dogs, the basic premise lost among weeds
by the river like the time we struck out
for the mountains on rumors of gold, the big mules
loaded down with equipment
and someone up ahead singing a song about
love's fits and smashups, the way we told ourselves
there'd be another chance, the grandeur we always depended on,
and beauty, they said, our true love, like a reference
to small time game preserves where the operators
herded the animals into thickets
and far fields the customers could never find
and there set up tents and offered free vittles
as if the arrangement met some kind of standard theretofore
unpracticed in the country where most
were only the tarnished trophies of those for whom the get-go
was just another way of saying the doctor is not in.

MAXIMUS, MINIMUS
~ Ron Smith

Jaundiced Clement conducted
the ceremony himself, joining
fourteen-year-old Caterina to
the third creation of the Duke
of Orléans, then shuffled off
to Rome to die—which great city
threw the party prodigious, one
Roman running a sword through
the dead pope's entrails, another
changing "Clemens Pontifax
Maximus" to "Inclemens Pontifex
Minimus." History is silent
about Caterina's grief, glee.
Only that liar Cellini claimed
to have wept, claimed to have
kissed the little yellow feet, cold
as St. Peter's. That is to say
Cambio's graceless St. Peter,
which you can still kiss today,
the one with the toes worn
smooth by the lips of the pious.

MYNDDAEG HOUR
~Lisa Russ Spaar

Mind-day, old word
for the year's turning

over horizon's sable pew,
just words left, then,

time already thinning.
What is not God's day?

But this is ours.
Let's save our souls

for later, in favor
of the body's disguises,

bell-pull spine, fisted hair,
heart's buried clock.

In another kind of tale,
a glass shoe might dandle in your hand,

a future, on bent knee.
Unshod desire, instead,

steps out when we're old
in the names of fur, toenails,

wren the nest becomes.
That voltage. How not die?

We will. Fawn felled by the roadside
on the drive home. We're her bride.

WROUGHT
~ Jane Springer

& there were many separations of land from land.

Many mansions' wrought iron fences staked claim on the ground
so adjacent chainlinks seemed fragile nets of mist.

Phonewires wound in clear sight, then went fugitive in vegetation.

Gravel banked our tracks, craters held wet light by the River called
Hudson.

We didn't understand why 2x4s boxed mature trees, PVC joints
flocked mown pasture.

Sometimes a factory, sometimes a park—one angled, the other lay
a concrete runners' arc beside receptacles of trash.

Topiaries made one town cute—another sprung backlots, graffiti
blubbed slabs, spent slugs.

Wherever long rushes went uninterrupted, blue heron dive-bombed
fish or forsythias yellowed slate cliffs.

If the bodies drifting platforms between stations had been unclothed
they would, as animals, have sloped beautiful in various skins.

In the space between cars, you could stick your arm into wind. That's
where the conductor told

how awful it was for the engineer when the elderly couple parked
their truck against the way of freight—No way, he said, not to look.

In the river, driftwood, rebar, flag on a pier's end. Having had neither
painter's century, nor gentle brush

a Space Alien beside us sang kathunk, doowah, shoo. Of what is iron
made? Earth. Of what—the litter & blooms, of what so

what, she uncoupled herself from judgment or use—a watcher
unpained by temporal connection.

> So we searched her bag—
> but found no coin worth purchase.
> So we rent her garments
> & made pretty train
> curtains

> & she didn't seem to care we
> cut her hair—a new material
> for fiddle bows we
> hoped would not
> give out.

Space Alien, I can't reach your origin of spherical & blameless
music fast enough, if it weren't for ocular love,

I do—

Riverdale & Wave Hill were the real names of towns we passed
through. It's eons since we buried mother at the Natural

History Museum & of her face only the essence remains peach
pale pink rose bark bitter shapes shifting dark brown tan gray
wheel going soft flesh the haunted house of the missing
hair pick Someone's banjo riffs unraveled plunked
notes fingers touch blind touch—if you want

Love you will have to batter past eden
& believe there was no order gar-
den hoe or walleye fish we saw
less felt more no man made
name we no jasmine hold
or celadon jug no ochre
rudder rust root flame
& limitless colorless
hammerless no first
last anvil's fall once
weren't we just

      volume

  plush

full-tilt

    then
          space?

What the engineer couldn'a seen: The old man smelled like the bait
shop that morning. She'd just whispered the most startling,

beautiful thing.

HOOK
~ Page Hill Starzinger

To
    hang
        from heels,
            24 articulating
          vertebrae
    falling
into their own

curves, this
    backbone—
        same
            for swans
        as sloth.
    Dangling
thread

of *bored young men*
and *beautiful deer*, they called her,
who *vanished*,
did not respond
for article
headlined *Gang Rape, Routine and Invisible*.
Is one surprised. Now
reporting:
Huh is the only
universal
human word, not
mama, as linguistics believed. Especially
as Ms. Tarlton emerges
with a new face stitched to her scalp
after her husband beat her with a baseball bat,

227

soaked her with industrial lye squirted from a dish soap bottle.
A spinous process, downward and backward
to the sacral
pelvic girdle.
Atlas and axis aligning, like a
bow spring—

THE TERRACES AGAINST THE HILLSIDE SAY IMMORTAL, THE TREES—
~ Terese Svoboda

The terraces say whatever they say, decay really, less Man was here
than the tree, cabled to the hillside, the blue of eternity laid between

each needle. Beyond me and the little construct of time and space
I occupy, eating eating eating, my infrared heat, my several single-
    celled selves

exchanging parasites in the ether around skin and cough and spoor
is the trunk, with its deceit of root and branch belying its age,

leaning on the bare cable. Its evergreen bows never go bare
and the wind against them never dies. The more sophisticated

argue that the cable's current is equally tree, and so is the smoke at night
that makes me weep, the shed needles in their beds, and the intricate sea.

Two for the Road
~ Brian Swann

I: House of Cards:

Cards aren't meant to make you happy. In fact, it often seems just the opposite. You can read *The Living End* as much as you want but there's no secret there for the real card-worker to learn. Sure you can "pick a card" simply by naming the card held in someone's hand, but what if you are face down among a group of cards that are similarly oriented? It is all a question of fluid symmetry, sensing what's what. This is how one achieves authority and reputation. As for any impromptu take-a-card endings that require little or no skill, simply turning a card over will not be a sufficiently memorable conclusion. To be a myriad-cardician requires demanding sleights. Close-up mysteries facilitate one's transition from pasteboard presto to impromptu self-working. This way you make a surprise impact even on yourself, becoming your own traveling ace no non-specialist can fathom. But what is revealed is no dodge, if properly understood. It is genuine mastery of the internal, executing oneself in a flawless pass, disappearing in a flicker of stratagems, all meat and no fat, a one-handed shuffle from one place to another like a flourish of fanning mirrors, a flounce off the top of the deck where all can see. This is how you give an alternative to routine with the appearance of no difficulty. You bypass the predictable, passing unreal mysteries through real holes in the universe.

II: Topit:

Your actual contribution is quite minimal. But with it you can predict
a word or even a passage, even one that has been secretly selected. This
can leave the foundation for learning even more sophisticated tricks,
sometimes including quite large objects. Sometimes too the insides of
a building can be revealed by means of psychology or good guesswork.
Concomitantly, vanishing becomes resurrection inside-out. It can be
done via household objects, creating a domestic eye-view of eternity
that can eventually lead to a bird's eye view. Even the most insightful
theoretician can never teach us how to reach into a hat and come up
with anything not already in existence. Any lecture notes turn out to
be hocus-pocus. But when the hocus-pocus turns out to be the main
supply-house then we have the performance performing itself. So, a
typical spectator is unnecessary, no more than a hypothesis when other
yeasty factors are at work, the way the unseen can have spectacular
unseen events. A natural bonding takes place, a self-transcendence
where misdirection can take the place of real dexterity. Eventually the
need for patter diminishes as the hats begin to fly with no visible means
of propulsion. This is chapeaugraphy at its best and most convincing.
Soon heads will fly too. This is the soul's evolving choreography. This is
the topit absorbed and going without saying.

THE SIXTH WALK
~ Cole Swensen

took place entirely on a bridge.   It brought within it   things in which
I was alone. So there I was, looking down on the tops of trees looking

down on wind. In fact, a form of window I couldn't bear to cross. All
night is a way of walking   of rocking with the dark.   A closer look

brought the headlights out—a cortège winding its way through the park
far below. My guide on its own, and I, hounded, bear the sway.   (She

likens it to waking amid the detritus of an enormous feast, they feasted

into morning, and, indeed, at dawn   the animals began their crossings
careful not to disturb   my silence, and occasionally, a child. I am used to it

now   and now I think of it as a painting   of a woman opening her mail.

TRANSFIGURATIONS
~ Arthur Sze

Though neither you nor I saw flowering pistachio trees
in the Hanging Gardens of Babylon, though neither
you nor I saw the Tigris River stained with ink,
though we never heard a pistachio shell dehisce,
we have taken turns holding a panda as it munched
on bamboo leaves, and I know that rustle now.
I have awakened beside you and inhaled August
sunlight in your hair. I've listened to the scroll
and unscroll of your breath—dolphins arc along
the surface between white-capped waves; here,
years after we sifted yarrow and read from the *Book
of Changes*, I mark the dissolving hues in the west
as the sky brightens above overhanging willows.
The panda fidgets as it pushes a stalk farther
into its mouth. We step into a clearing with budding
chanterelles; and, though this space shrinks and
is obscured in the traffic of a day, *here* is the anchor
I drop into the depths of teal water. I gaze deeply
at the panda's black patches around its eyes;
how did it evolve from carnivore to eater of bamboo?
So many transfigurations I will never fathom.
The arc of our lives is a brightening then dimming,
brightening then dimming—a woman catches
fireflies in an orchard with the swish of a net.
I pick an open-mouthed pistachio from a bowl
and crack it apart: a hint of Assyria spills
into the alluvial fan of sunlight. I read spring in
autumn in the scroll of your breath; though
neither you nor I saw the completion of the Great Wall,
I wake to the unrepeatable contour of this breath.

FROM *DOWNSTREAM*
~ Daniel Tobin

Twelve voice retablos after twelve paintings of Eleanor Spiess-Ferris

I. *LISTENING*

How long have I been sleeping here
Naked upon this louche divan, fluid
In my sloping dream, the dream I dream
Of you in the terracotta shadows
Listening? I might be an odalisque,
Though this is no one's chamber but my own,
And yours—it is the chamber of the dream
In which I speak to you, the faintest breath
Out of Brahma's mouth, say, the fragrance
Of lotus drifting across the waters,
Or the scent of a word that comes to know
Its meaning by moving dream to dream.
I have been sleeping here a long long time.

II. *RIVER*

When I rose from the river I was still
The river, and in my red hair flamed
The encircling wheels, wheels within wheels,
By which the very air around me moved.
It was then I felt my body blossom
Orchid and trumpet flower, lily and lace,
A necklace of birds spread hand to hand
As my fingers poised to key them into song:
To be the stream and what allays the stream—
Fountain plash, dolphin leap, supernova sky.
And the nipple-hard blue mantle of my breast
Like a cold eye staring into nothing.

LAMENT
~ translated by Jay Hopler

Sleep and death, the bleak eagles,
Beat their wings about this head all night long:
Eternity's icy wave washes away
Man's golden image. The purple body
Is smashed to pieces on the spine-
Chilling reefs, and the dark voice
Grieves over the sea.
Sister Stormy Melancholy,
Look: a fearful boat sinks
Beneath the stars,
The silent face of night.

KLAGE
~ original by Georg Trakl

Schlaf und Tod, die düstern Adler
Umrauschen nachtlang dieses Haupt:
Des Menschen goldnes Bildnis
Verschlänge die eisige Woge
Der Ewigkeit. An schaurigen Riffen
Zerschellt der purpurne Leib.
Und es klagt die dunkle Stimme
Über dem Meer.
Schwester stürmischer Schwermut
Sieh ein ängstlicher Kahn versinkt
Unter Sternen,
Dem schweigenden Antlitz der Nacht.

WELCOME HOME
~ William Trowbridge

Large sign in many American ports at the end of WWII

All I have is a black-and-white photo,
taken in our yard, my father holding me,
him still in his khakis, me dwarfed
beneath his service cap, both of us
looking as if the other might bite,
warrior and war baby joined
by biology and chance, him smiling
stiffly for Mother's camera. He brought
souvenirs—his bayonet, a Nazi pistol—
and a taste for Luckies, bourbon,
and rage. When he hugged, his cheek
scraped like sandpaper, how I thought
a hero's face should feel; his slaps
could blur my eyes.

They say three months in combat
fractures a normal mind. He'd spent
almost a year, the details of which
would stay off-limits. We must have
looked like aliens, my mother, sister,
and I, so plump and washed and green,
our neighborhood hospitable as Mars.
Welcome home, one of the Martians
must have said.

HANDWRITING'S ANCESTORS
~ Chase Twichell

When I took over Dad's finances
I read his check register's

minuscule marginal notes
(many question marks, lists of groceries).

He was living on *the soup that eats like a meal.*
We had to drive him home when his

key wouldn't fit in the radio.
No one could stop

the slow truck of brain damage.
His last letters canted, diminutive

script written as if uphill, petering out
or running off the edge of the page.

Sometimes a tautness enters my hand,
so that my writing becomes slightly

more angular, smaller, with
'shrunken' and 'crabbed' in its near future.

Dad's handwriting enters mine
as frost takes the ground.

AFTER THE INVENTION OF POLYSTYRENE A LIGURIAN GOAT CROSSES THE EQUATOR
~ Marc Vincenz

Abut in a tailspin, mad spark
of keratin scratching hard-
wood—and that buck-

toothed back-bite, double-
chew driving through
everything if-you-pleases:

shoes, hats, buttons, ties—
that crumpled trilby Giuseppe wore
with his '30s Valentino, and

in the buttonhole, an off-
white carnation—in another incarnation,
carrying the fleas of late middle age—;

an idler, a swiller of leftover
orange pop, a guzzler
of misconstrued rubbish, gunk and grease—

'*sono malcontento e raccattaticcio,*'
as was parlayed
by Great Uncle Fabrizzio

before his last hand of blackjack
on an ocean liner
from Jakarta to Genoa via Dar es Salaam

as he observed an empty
can of mystery meat circle
a lone polystyrene container,

then hover and dive gullishly
into a shoal of mackerel
in a calm whaleless Indian Ocean

crossing the equatorial
with a borderline heart attack
—and finally, that Bornean warrior,

not raised by Cain, but a clan
of cannibals, a bird's delicate leg bone
through his flared nostrils, adjusting

his penis sheath on the crux
of an equinox while dreaming
of a creature he'd never seen

but knew from a lifetime of belly-
aches and breathy sighs, curried
in Bombay on a street stall

in sinews and gristle, fat-
dripping to a chuffed-
up floor, dusted in fine particles

of a most ancient Macedonian gold
collected mote by mote on fingertips
by a team of orphaned ragamuffins

known as the 'All That Glitters'—and
that mad pan-flute-playing
Italian passione that carried

Uncle Fabrizzio from the silver
platter of bright colonial Indonesia
to the shredded and shaded

alleys of serpentine Genoa
in pursuit of a dream of old wives' tales
more than anything he could have foreseen.

VIEW FROM THE BACKYARD
~ Marc Vincenz

A brief metallic sound:
keys upon coins and coins upon keys.
She's saying just do it—and,

it's not acidic like some well-inclined logo
ticked for athletic shoes, at least not
until the afterburn quietens

in the inner view—but there is a problem;
these matches are damp and although
she would love to ignite before the dusk,

she already blazes luminescent, exudes
a whiff of adolescence in her wild spray
of indigo blooms. And I hesitate

to let this cigarette tumble, to witness
all this youth go poof in blinding smoke
that waters. Even these crinkled wrappers

and dented cans smack of romance
in our bold designated light, nuzzling
each other like concerned lovers. Behind

the man-holed chicken wire, torn
from hinges, seething, the defensive
warehouse glares—and from nowhere

a soul sensed, not a single woman pushing
a responsibility, not a lone child spinning
wheels, not even a rat's determined squeak

to disturb this angular indifference. Honestly:
What *is* the sound of citizens walking
in a new age of supple soles?

CHILD LOST IN THE NIGHT
~ Santiago Vizcaíno, translated by Alexis Levitin

One doesn't know if behind the rainbow of
the world there isn't a stain of blood.

Suddenly one is relaxed,
one romps upon a pleasure too rewarding,
one tries to smile,
with dissimulation,
so a certain stupidity will not confound itself with happiness.

And one even believes they have given back one's old route,
the right direction.
One makes plans,
begins to walk with the air of a leopard.
One breakfasts conscientiously,
peoples the carpet with pyramids,
and brings along one's spiders.

But the cry of the mother brings back my fear,
the crown of horror on the nape of my neck.
I run as if I were alive,
with the lightness of the octopus not yet touched by the net.
I think that they mistook my nest,
that they couldn't tear away, just like that,
the illusion of changing one's course,
that they couldn't fuck up one's hope of seeing oneself in another body,
of sharing features, gestures,
and even a way of saying papa.

They couldn't say to someone, damn it all,
no one is guilty,
the night I used to hiding its miracles and its deaths.

Forget that I'm the last being in this world.
Forget that my guide is an olive tree about to die.
But don't embrace me as you gaze at me.
Don't confuse your scorn with your pity.
Forget that I'm the last being in this world.

Suddenly one adjusts,
goes back to cleaning one's face with floor polish,
and, in the middle of all the confusion, hears someone say:
"When you lose a son, you also lose your fatherhood."

62 MILES (THE ATMOSPHERE) NOT 7,926 MILES (THE EARTH)
~ Arthur Vogelsang

The atmosphere is thin, by a happy accident,
Around the fat ball of the planet.
This is us.

I thought I would celebrate
Since it seems a system that's going on
Close enough to forever.

Imagine if your tires
Were six feet tall.
You'd break your frigging leg
Just getting out, so they're two feet tall.

That's a system that works.
Imagine if the atmosphere was as thick
As the fat planet—compare stats in title above,
Not 62 miles of air, but 7,926 miles of air!

You'd need some set of lungs for that.

You wouldn't be able to squeeze your chest through
Your bedroom doorway, your bathroom doorway,
We'd have to have something else besides portals.

We'd need huge shirts.

We'd need thick steel helmets growing out of flesh
Against the pressure of 7,296 miles of air pressing
On us. We'd have to dress as knights.
Think of seven billion knights, among them baby knight suits.

Instead lightly covered by only air and clothes
We go on in some kind of endless axis
As if an axis could be endless!

Or we sail around something which sails around something
And the numerous curves expand close to forever

Even on cloudy days and eventually the sun will be merciless.

GENOVA SUPERBA
~ Karen Volkman

Med head—lozenges and drops—keep it talking
what's that pressure in the legs
descending from ears

"the sea's incoherences"
she says, but it was she
and not the sea

in the shell-skull
making waves
we weren't hearing. Si si, ok,

time's a waste, time's
a-wasting, and it's a matter of taste,
professor bluefish

why buy three when you can
get six, and watch them slit open
with the heads on

but mine
is full of zones
and omens, I don't think

you walk so fast
or it's more urban,
inventing banking

was inspiration
for the pesto,
correct?

Or an anchovy
looks me in the eye
saying stroke my spine

ticklish fish
bright funicular
swims out/in

I mind

Brioche; or, Try to Remember, Diane, the Laws of Thermodynamics You Studied in Physics All Those Years Ago
~ Diane Wakoski

matter or energy never lost)

When I think of loss, I am usually as bitter
as lemons, scorched
coffee, or perhaps
an unripe plum, unless
it's today when I unpacked and discovered
my zippered black leather jewelry case was missing:
    lost, the silver and onyx floral chain, deceptively simple;
    a starlight-burst slivered-silver spiky necklace—
        both pricey gifts from Robert;
    lost, modest early amber, another gift from Robert, a pale-ale-colored
        cabochon, embraced by beveled silver,
        hanging with slim rectitude
        on a very thin platinum chain;
    lost, my collection of earrings for the trip:
        tiny teapot crystal earrings that tip and seem to
        invite you to pour;

hanging poker hands, royal flushes, against black, circled with gold—
these both, imaginative gifts from a poet who calls herself
a punk Persephone;
inexpensive but new/Lady of Light onyx elegance;
my favorite subtle, lucent aquamarine tears,
clasped with burnished silver—

also a gift, these
from a world-traveller friend
of forty years;
beveled jade squares hanging below a copper bead—each
stone crafted by a heartbreakingly sad funny
poet and made to catch my chi;
amber teardrops such as a goddess might weep,
another early present Robert found
at our local antique store;

lost, only one bracelet, since I am old and seldom wear them
anymore/it was a wire-thin gold bangle,
a present from a poet who was young
fifty years ago;

what I will miss most—odd, I thought of it last—
the gold and freshwater pearl necklace Robert
gave me/I call it my "Tin-cup" necklace
because Renee Russo wore one like it in that movie,

now lost and gone with it,
the hanging pearl drop earrings,
also given to me by punk Persephone;
memory has hidden pockets, and I just realized that in the bottom
of one of the sleeves of the jewelry case was a stickpin/
decorated with an enameled star,
looking like a faery wand,
given to me by a colleague who said,
"Diane, I think
you are a star."

Today my loss is similar to aging—
I feel winded, as if from a long run.
Breathing hard,
catching my breath:
how in life
possessions are like
especially attractive food and today
will think
of my lost jewelry as a good meal.
Perhaps, four courses, such as:

a *paté en croute*, picholine olives, some *cornichons*

white asparagus served with a sauce of raspberries

steak, *frites* (my favorite)

gâteau opéra, with its tiny insignia of gold
          on each piece

I'd drink sparingly,
only one glass for the whole meal,
my current favorite a red Zinfandel from an Italian
winery in Sonoma, California.
What I have lost is like the meal—inside me.

Or perhaps, the lost jewelry is only
a cup of tea and a brioche,
something small,
a refreshment. After all, the jewelry itself
is somewhere beyond me, lying in its
bible-black case. I am old and
      trying to teach myself loss, Of
          course, still yearning,
though today has me thinking
        pears,
         grapes, not

feeling citrus-y or bitter,
(physics, Diane, matter or energy never lost)
my jewelry
not lost, only gone somewhere else.

JONES MOUNTAIN ECLOGUE
~ G. C. Waldrep

First hard freeze. Night for the setting of traps. So what
if the dialogue was about sexual possession, in the end? Apophony,
plasmic trinity of sound moving away
from the body. And why must we use honey, you asked.
Because it is expensive and because it scathes the soul, I replied.
We could hear dead voices in the distance.
That which is sweetness corrects for that which is death.
No I would never value the roses more than Christ, I thought.
(Because what if the dialogue is about sexual possession, in the end?)
Because it is my name day and I am very tired.
First hard freeze. Night of warnings and recriminations.
The honey she sent me, from across an ocean. Its brittle vial.
Because my mother called to remind me what the weather was like
while she lay in the hospital giving birth to me,
to my body. A rhetorical form that concedes sleep's shapeliness.
I can't remember the name of that place I want to *stay*,
she kept saying. While knives were distributed to children.
I test my breath on the lathe of the night air; it hums.
So, "the merciless recurrence of our nakedness" (Ann Lauterbach).
But we were brought here by such splendid vanities, I protested.
The Christ for which Nineveh waited. The errancy.
Spread before the congregation like swaths of ivory chenille.
It is not that we are possessed, but that some vagrance hunts us.
And then what had been my soul leapt within me,
exultant. Each of the stars in the cemetery raises its five-
fingered fraction to me. We are all coffins for your scent, they sing.
I'm burned from listening to them, the tender flesh
of my inner ears shines with scars. I am afraid
of sleep's charcoal sketch. If only I could give my blood away,
I murmured to the winter hives. The native name

for this mirror is breath, my physician insists. First hard
freeze, first glass tone. I go to him carrying my cities in my hands.

RUIN PORN
~ Rosanna Warren

Thy silver is become dross ...
Isaiah 1: 22

At the 59TH St. Metra station, the walls
are streaked with black and viridian mold
and stucco falls from crowded columns as
from an abandoned Turkish bath.
Sound of dripping water; leaves like dead mice;
broken glass; ticket window hammered over with plywood.
I came looking for lost clues. But Beauty Supply,
hawked by a shop down the street, is in short supply.
Your country is desolate, your cities are burned with fire.
I looked for myself in a puddle: my face was smeared.
Enter into the rock, o.k., but trains
still wheeze to the rickety wooden platform
chewed out by salt. Carp float belly-up
in the ornamental Japanese pond in the nearby park,
their sequins blurred, their silver become dross.
Honey locusts planted along the lake
have strewn the scurf with leather bookmark pods:
the codex is smudged, the binding torn,
and no one reads that archaic script any more.

FROM *EIGHT TRIGRAM SPIRIT BOXING*
Afaa Michael Weaver

Photograph by Rachel Eliza Griffiths

EIGHT TRIGRAM SPIRIT BOXING
THE WHEELS INSIDE THE WHEELS
–Afaa Michael Weaver 蔚雅風

The Sears and Roebuck Roadmaster was my beautiful bicycle. When I learned to take the rear axle apart to lubricate the ball bearings, I thought I was ready to design space ships. I took the axle apart carefully, laying the pieces out in the backyard such that I knew the order of the reassembly. We were the black southern working class transported to a relatively northern Baltimore. When I landed in the Bethlehem steel mill alongside my uncles in 1970, after two years at the University of Maryland in College Park, the most sophisticated mechanical work I did was to follow giant electric cranes as a helper. I was there for a year and at Procter & Gamble for fourteen years to do the same work, to service the machines that kept the world's largest economic market full to the brim with things. I have the working-class blues, which is not sadness but the realm of a music and poetics that is more than the literal blues. It is a holy dance that I have come to see as Chinese spirit boxing.

In my office in academia, the memories visit me. In a milli-second I am punching the time clock in the tin mill of Bethlehem steel mill in Sparrows Point, just over the city line into Baltimore County. I pass the loud whir of the high speed shears, and there are shouts from men calling to one another. I get closer to the far end of the mill where raw tin is pressed flat and shiny and the smell thickens. Men drive electric tow motors that are one story tall. It's the industrial world I know must be the model for sci-fi films, which is why, I suppose, that I come back again and again to that genre. The industrial world is what industrial engineers designed so that factories would be perfect machines and the humans in them made to work like machines so as to ensure that perfection. It was to improve the world and to make colossal piles of money for the privileged. The rich are richer and we have the smartphone.

Memory works such that if we think backwards from inside a thought to retrieve the thought that preceded it, we may not locate that preceding thought but instead find ourselves immediately confronting the paradox of history. Reaching from the present into the past is, in reality, a fool's errand, even with digital cameras and recorders everywhere, and there is no technology for recording thought as it appears in the mind. This is the space where poetry is born and where it has dominion. Poetry stands to defy the machine.

The poems I've been honored to have featured here in *Plume* are from a manuscript entitled *Eight Trigram Spirit Boxing*. I am traveling to a world that no longer exists, and as I move forward or backward or deeper inside the space between what was then, what is now, and what can be, I keep in mind that this may be another world for some readers. I learned to live in that world and to escape it with knowledge contained in the Chinese art of Taijiquan and its Daoist influences. Among the sayings of the masters in the art, there is the idea that at advanced levels the body is moved by the spirit, and I like to think of this as a kind of holy dance I knew as a child in black churches.

I believe the spirit holds a truth for us beyond the world of machines, and that truth is protected, nurtured by poetry through which I am hoping to articulate my working class blues, the spirit's dance according to what I know and am learning about Chinese culture.

蔚雅風

BEATITUDES, THE PEACEMAKERS

If a brother has killed folk in war,
he is one of the quiet ones at work,

sitting with his coffee and lunch,
patting the floor with his foot,

waiting for the joke he can't make
right now but is working on inside

a memory, peeling away the scars
to find the innocence underneath,

ribbons of what was done blessed
by God & Country, the corporation

with a seal made in ungodly heaven,
where wars are all there is. Inside

is now this space with all of us,
some of us who killed folk at home,

some by accident, or by mean intent,
plans made when forgiving failed.

Still others who have not killed
strut like cocks on the walkway

to trophies they can never have,
and all the while there are the few

who fear even the talk of war, who
make the jokes and fetch the coffee,

who take the butts of jokes, who run
when running is what makes us one,

as brother with brother, not bound
by blood or love but what we must do.

BEATITUDES, THE MERCIFUL

A white man born in coal country,
George knew the power of dirt,
what dirt can do, raise you up a mess
of vegetables in a season of kindness
between the hard edge of the hills, a gift
for the hungry. A white man born where
not much grows, he knew the dirt of work,
of chasing Rommel across the Sahara,
taking hot showers with gasoline.

He knew to be grateful for having lived
a soldier and come home mostly whole,
meeting me for our afternoon coffee,
our blue shirts, our blue pants, our blues
in five notes—
　　　　You need that five dollars, Mike?

To give me what he needed more than me,
I took the five and gave it back seven days
from the first day of the week, back again
for coffee, back again for what is not free,
our blues the five notes of this ritual—
　　　　Here's your five back, George. Thanks.
　　　　Need it again, Mike? Just say the word.

A black man born in a steel city knows
the power of dirt, how hard things
come out of it, go back, back into earth
where dirt is the clean thing of a world,
a mercy seat for men who love kindness,
five dollars going back and forth until
a day men are not only clean but free.

WHEN THEY FIRED OUR MAGICIAN

It was the day the FM rock station died,
back when they threatened to replace us
with robots to obey what we ignored.

It was a day when sunlight filled the yard
with trucks in every other door, not full
or empty just what makes this our work,

we taking the chance to be at ease, slide
to hidden places in the warehouse to read
what kept us, first of the month porno,

Hustler, Playboy, the Zane Grey novels,
the one book of poetry, and his mystery,
theosophy, unseen worlds only magicians

see with eyes that know the inner spaces,
galaxies inside the mundane wheels, floors
made of cement, windows of chicken wire,

the body of this, our prison he ignored
with chocolate milk, Madame Blavatsky,
cheese and biblical codes for the occult,

his science of metaphysical conundrums,
honing the skill of traveling across history
while stacking soap, taking his time to get

to work, to come back from break, zen
walker, koan breaker, soul speaker of souls
so abrupt in being the oasis of us he was

taken away with the pink slip of paper,
a proverb of absence, that last day a shout
from the rebellion he took with him.

THE GOOD TRAVELER

> *Good travelers leave no tracks.*
> —*Laozi* 27

It lives in me, the trucker's bathroom
off to the side when you walk the walkway,
the old German church refusing to move,

along the walkway to the warehouse door
windows where the clerks bend over sheets,
counting trucks, counting hours, counting,

the warehouse door open sometimes to us
pushing pallets into trucks, easing tow motors
like square yellow Cadillacs or bumper cars,

machines replacing machines, the carousel
with its computer filling what was a conveyor,
the carousel that was to be the first of robots

taking over from our sloth, then the shorter
walkway to the door leading to the upstairs
where the managers schemed in white shirts,

with us downstairs, around the bend where
the closet sat, the janitor's keeping place,
leading to the rec room where we took

time away in the clatter of repetition,
axis of everything we had, the round
tables for cards, lunch, *Guns & Ammo*,

Daily Racing Form, the leather Bible
to admonish the thoughts we think so we
can try to stay connected with what is alive,

ping-pong table in the back, we the stars
who shone beyond tournaments, our fridge
next to the time clock secured with bolts

in the wall, the wall secured to us, locked
to the treasury miles away printing money
the way we fill these empty trucks, origins

not something our kind should doubt,
as sure as the vending machines across
the room from the microwave that came

soon after Raiders of the Lost Ark, or
Star Wars, whichever was first to imagine
the spaces we kept open for imagination,

sleeping in the bathroom or washing up
in the round fountain next to the mirror,
next to the toilets scrubbed free of shit,

while upstairs the white shirts think
what men with intelligence think, not
what we know, diamonds that we are.

Laozi *translated by Stephen Addiss & Stanley Lombardo*

IVORY SOAP, A WHITENESS

In the hot houses the soap waits
in innocence, purely white, soft, hard,

cut up from the long tubes of ooze
from the vats where men sweat in globs

to earn the cleanliness of saints, washing
souls like the Akan priests, sage work,

Adams letting the Eves fall from them,
Eves gathering dust to make the Adams,

all histories writ and rewritten anew,
again and again, the company awash

in profitable hallelujahs. I open the door,
let the steam of Ivory soap whiteness

fill me to take the trays to Marty, whose
work is to feed the bars to the machine

that stamps the logo, guarantees the purity
of the company stamp, bosses of America's

dirt watching to see that the machines
do not rest from the perfect form of bars

of soap sliding down the rubber belts,
under sprays of salty water, into the metal

stamp plates where hot sealers brand soap's
flesh, while Marty, Aikido master of the line,

stops to tell me the details of Russia
from his last summer vacation, to ask

my opinion on Islam, the Arab slave trade,
the business of taking the masters' names,

while the motor pulls the rubber belts
full of bars of our redemption, little bricks,

whiteness marching out to stores to wash
away the sluggish shame of being dirty,

cash registers counting the money we make
for masters who sit in invisible places,

designing our wages, what wages can buy,
while men like my father, black, white,

brown, yellow bodies aching with work
from mills and the holds of filthy ships at sea

dream what it takes to make life in a nation
obese with forgetting, hungry for what is new.

A selection from Eight Trigram Spirit Boxing *by Afaa Michael Weaver*

KNOWLEDGE OF SILK

> *Look at plain silk; hold uncarved wood.*
> *The self dwindles; desires fade.*
> *Laozi* 19

If you really want to know think about wanting to do something
while you in the wrong place for doing it, reading a book on company
time, taking naps at night cause you worn out from trying to get all
your shit done in time so you can read a little western philosophy
before the bosses come in the morning, understanding the bosses
think you some low life and you know you ain't because you went
to university some, too, and you ain't the only one among you, or
wanting to sit on the steps at the college and eat lunch when you
finish trying to teach the chirrun, most of em white and you black
as blue black can be because we made that way in Baltimore, where
black folk been as long as there been this America, and my peoples
come from slavery and wanting to say all of that to students who
never been this close to a black man, me in the classroom hearing
the sounds of machines, riding to Sparrows Point with a driver
sipping on his morning vodka, taking the turn to the mills, all of em
a bunch of smokestacks with my daddy's face on it, me now knowing
what pains he had all over his soul just to make a paycheck next
to white folks who wouldn't talk to him, under white folk who
thought workers is all low life, then me with the white supervisor
who was proud I wrote poetry and wanted to help me, the good
with the bad, the crooked with the straight, me knowing work
without a proper place, and no place proper and my proper the way
I like it in a world that still don't know things ain't never gonna
be right until we can love a piece of steel without making it be
something, and know the machines have to stop … one happy day.

Laozi *translated by Stephen Addiss & Stanley Lombardo*

THE BLUESMAN SPEAKS ON ORIGINAL MAN

The hook in his hand, lifting the metal plate,
smacking down the crevice of truck and dock,
he went on about the way folk looked at first,

at first when the dew of Eden was still wet
on the nipples of young lovers, and a perfect
order like the well loaded trucks full of soap

was in the air everywhere, angels sitting
around in trees like it was natural, and it all
was natural, Bluesman easing into his gloves,

hands that knew Richmond, Spartansburg,
Roanoke Rapids, the February southern spring,
hands that done wrung out grief over folk lost

in the undertow of life, he spoke from deep
in the black blue of being baptized in rivers,
and whispering songs to women at night

about the sweet and dirty ole love, a slight
aberration he said, something God required
of the blues, and he went on about the first

appearance of the human beings, how they
ain't had no color, how color was not natural
on the tongue of God, how color was the idea

of angels who fell out the trees one night,
drinking gin, laughing at the Lord, taking
the law to be some kind of plaything, a toy,

while the sky turned over and rolled up,
sick in its stomach the way only the sky can be,
and the sun began to throw anger on folk

who had been designed to see no difference
between themselves, the Bluesman explained,
on a day when color filled the truck yard,

seagulls some kind of dirty gray and white,
the rolled eyes of tired truck drivers blue, brown,
and hazel, arms white, dirty white, golden brown,

ashy black, throats dry and thirsting for beer,
hearts all red and some near done with fatigue,
this color, this thing the Bluesman said was what

the doctors would say is an occlusion, his hands
wiping his eyes as if he was weeping, but smiling,
singing, turning boxes up, stacking them with

their own weight, ringing out truth's raw gospel.

JOHN HENRY SLEEPING IN HIGH GRASS

Mowers miles away, horse flies on top
his hammer like they own it, his chest
cresting and falling in shapes shifting
between sunlight and leaves, black steel
his destiny, John is motion at rest,
tides of moon and waves in still waters,
suns igniting hearts of molten iron,
a hardened conviction, rose petals in rain.

Sleep is a dream, the real world a poundage,
work a sentence for being his mama's son,
the hammer in his crib, the supernatural

a drum song of woodpeckers, cow bells
in the field, heaven a home going back to
a place before the bugle call to be born.

THE WINEPRESS

Men and women come new, fresh,
step into one end of the mills dancing,
come out the other hobbling, coughing

up the accumulated frustrations
of paychecks eating away at paychecks,
loan sharks promising to realize dreams.

Steel mills chew up workers,
put the young flesh in their jaws,
teeth shining with ads for things.

The miracles the beaten houses built
for workers in master plans, paychecks
enough to get you to the job, to stand

in line for overtime, great leaps forward
on the backs of twenty-four hour shifts,
living in the muffled sound of soot

lining your lungs, asbestos claiming
your place in cancer wards, prayers
heard and unheard, your children now

lined up around the bed, landscapes
workers become at the end of making
the wealthy rich, the children's grief

a wonder as you watch water on skin,
a sliding away, back to your youth
when work was a song, a deep prayer.

THE WORKER WE NAMED FREIGHT TRAIN & HIS REVELATION OF EZEKIEL'S VISION

In the stretched light of galaxies, the voice
broke through crusted skin of old scars, ridges
along valleys in the mountains of who he was.

He sang the song in a music sheet of star to star,
a harmony heard in the unseen world of wonder
some call heaven, some call a higher, hotter hell

than this world below, a man, a child, unhooked
from the false wings of his own thoughts to fly
into the brilliant fire of wheels, of God's tongue,

a gift he found in his eyes, not one some ache
to have, a gift too hot to handle, a gift crafted
to inspire envy should he live to mentor poets,

should he survive long enough to know the hand
on the heart. The grip on his soul was the hand
of the origin of life, wheels churning all time,

way past what any ego could hold, his mama
and daddy crying in the corner seeing him
blown wide open, the seraphim around him,

surgeons of air at the gurney handling organs
of a spirit given the hard road to sing the song
of workers and know the loneliness of Moses,

from the psych ward to the packing machines,
towers, unfilled boxes in tractor-trailers to live
among the sane as insane, to bring the vision

to their blind eyes of what waits for all of us.

HANDLING THE HEAVINESS

Conveyor wheels spin like the roller skates
we used in alleys, the whirring like a whistle,
boxes of soap coming down the line, inside
        the curve, the small ones
          the big ones—

one hundred pound boxes of Ivory like assassins
coming down the line for hand to hand combat,
and we fought—

      turning the box on itself, a shoulder
up in the air like a prayer lions make when they meet
their match, or the whistle of the hammer against
the steam engine, consumption laughing, knowing
it's what's gonna kill you—

      like the vodka swirling inside us,
          the cocaine, weed, pain killers

mixing the sweat with some kind of hysteria,
in the ring, bare knuckled against a bold Satan
for eight hours, nothing but your body to hold
you against the rot and stiffness that waits
when you retire …

keep me, O Lord, in the days of my youth,
hold me in this rocky space where life got
a hold on what time clocks want to steal

THE GOOD JOB

Illusions were first to go, then dreams,
weeks blanks filled minute by minute,
in crossword puzzles, staring into space,

risking hands and fingers in the mesh
of what keeps things going, what turns
Guiding Light and *Edge of Night*,

what pays bills and leaves extra money
to spend in shopping centers, the numbers
racket, or what the wiser of us do, save

for the day we will leave the good job
to go places we can't go now because
we have to save to go to those places,

and we are thankful for the job, after
illusions and dreams leave and we grow
up, grow into being tested. Questions

of whether we know what we really had
before we took the good job is a riddle
waiting to be a proverb while we count

how much true profit we can share with
something as big as outer space, we just
single pairs of eyes watching the product

roll by us, one box at a blessed time,
each space it travels a golden assurance
that we are paying for every sin we have.

BABY T
~ Charles Harper Webb

"When did we buy this turkey?" Drake asks Sheila.

"No idea," Sheila says.

The thing seems always to have been hunched in their freezer, inviolate as those Cuban cigars Drake's brother Stan, the Houston lawyer, bought, insured, and sealed in a thousand-dollar humidor.

"Maybe it's not a turkey," Sheila says. "Maybe, under all that ice, it's a chuck roast! We could have a crock-pot feast!"

"Maybe it's a kid," Drake says, "waiting to thaw out and be born. Baby T."

"Shhh!" Sheila orders. "Don't jinx me...."

Ice cream, orange juice, toast 'em waffles, and left-over spaghetti whisk through their freezer, shoving Baby T back to the rear. Ice thickens around it as, in Houston, Stan spins sexy cigar-fantasies.

"Please," his nicotine receptors call. "Oh, please ..."

"What the hell?" he finally says, and smokes one. Then, another. Then them all.

Baby T remains, a frozen planet in the dark of freezer-space, as Stan's cigars crumble to ash and, deep in Sheila's body, an egg drilled by a sperm begins to glow.

Sheila tells Drake, "We'll need a bigger house soon."

Emptying the freezer for the move, Drake finds the turkey buried like a stone ax in a cave. "My God," he says. "It's Baby T!"

"Don't call it that!" Sheila grips her bulge protectively. "Throw it away!"

Drake thinks how, consumed by regret, Stan birthed a lawsuit.

"Those cigars didn't *burn up*," opposing counsel cried. "You smoked them!"

"A fire's a fire," the judge declared, and ordered the insurance company to "make Stan whole."

"People eat 10,000-year-old mammoth dug from permafrost. They say it's good," Drake says, swaddling Baby T in newsprint for the drive to their new home.

        *   *   *

Too soon, their child finishes school, takes a job in Wichita, and leaves their house echoing with his loss.

"Why can't we start over?" Sheila sobs as they pack for Leisure World. "Maybe have a little girl …"

"Aging's the cruelest Crime Against Humanity," Drake groans, straining to lift their TV. "No way the law can make us whole."

This time, Sheila finds Baby T.

"Let's eat it," Drake says. "One last feast before we go!"

"No reason to take it with us," Sheila sighs, then hears, as if blown across white, frozen fields, an infant's cry.

COLLEGE OF BABIES
~ Charles Harper Webb

Did you think babies spill out of the womb knowing how to cry and mess their diapers, much less to babble, coo, and howl the whole night while their parents beg for sleep? No way! But people feel creepy if a newborn kips up, towels dry, stretches, and articulates, "How 'bout a blanket, Doc, before I freeze my keister?"

First Word, First Smile, First Step obsolete? Who'd stand for it?

The rare times a baby fails to endear itself to the world—won't toddle, say, or fuss; calls for the potty right away; writes, with crayon and butcher paper, "Barney sucks!"—people freak.

"Ignorant egghead," they rage. "Stupid fuckin' genius!"

BEING NERVOUS IS ONLY HUMAN
~ Dara Wier

You might be a chipped off edge of an Eggfly butterfly's wingtip
Tilted in the left-hand corner of a cracked aquarium
Sitting by a rusted dumpster behind an all night 7-Eleven
In an otherwise empty
Sickly lit parking lot. And it feels all right.
Without your eyespots you might be eaten alive.
Without your natural-born elements of deception.
Deception? What's deception to camouflage?
Contrition?
It's important to search for extraterrestrial intelligence.
Someplace else that we don't call ours.
A kind we can use.
A kind we might not recognize.
Otherwise, same old story, so what?
Being nervous is one way to pass the time.
Everyone always says they can't tell when you're nervous.
Proof of how badly it shows. Everyone knows that to affirm
a condition of nervousness residing as it does, mere centimeters
From prostration, —to affirm its existence has to be often forbidden.
We know everyone's intention amounts to being kind.
And we admit theses results in far better circumstances all the time.

Not Tonight,
~ Scott Withiam

she said. A truckload of rotten cantaloupes
dumped in a vacant lot behind the warehouses.
All that work and energy

to get it to a mass of featureless heads sinking
into one moldy mess. Who isn't
tempted to say *waste*, and let them go all the way,

keep walking? My neighbor: Sally.
Sally, as she always does, pulled something out of it:
a melon crate; wrenched it from that pile abuzz with bees.

Un-stung, she took it home dripping, hosed it down,
let it dry in the sun. Once dry, she covered it
with 'Blue Night' velour,

which, she said, always wants to be left
lustrous. "Leave it this way," she said,
stroking it, but I'm not sure on which stroke—

forwards or backwards—she left it.
I need to find out.
The velour she found years ago,

washed and put away until it spoke.
That was yesterday. It said, "This is the moment
I've been waiting for! I belong wrapped around the ribs

of that crate to make a nightstand."
That's how Sally talks, like "Pulled over and pulled down
tight around the crate then nailed down,

the crate won't wiggle.
Even stood on end, won't wobble."
Nor will her reading lamp,

placed upon the nightstand, move,
I thought, when I heard that.
She'll read in bed undisturbed

and at least the story she wants to read won't
be interrupted. But not tonight. Tonight it's hot,
and the wind blows. Her window remains open

and her lights are off, and I heard,
"You shouldn't be left flapping like that.
I'm putting you in a better place." She's talking

to a book.

OBSCURITY AND PROVIDENCE
~ C. D. Wright

The hand is immobilized

so the hand not usually in use

has to do all the work, has learned

to wait, to be quiet, to be still,

to receive memories; to tend

the fire; sometimes perceiving

a vague presence, the hand extends

in the perceived direction, retreats

pulls a sheet of paper from the drawer

that sticks, wet or dry;

scribbling fast at last, What

is he doing now, now that it is cold

where does he does he sleep.

When the dressing comes off

the smell is really pug.

PORTRAIT OF A HANGED WOMAN
~ Monica Youn

Now she could see that the air filling their rooms was supersaturated, thick with unspent silences. It was starting to precipitate out, the silences spinning themselves into filaments just below the surface of the visible. They drifted whitely upwards like seed-floss releasing from summer trees. They clustered together at the darkened ceilings of that house. They made no sound, of course—it would have been contrary to their nature—but sometimes she could feel a small pleased patterning of the air, like a cool current deep underwater. Over time they flourished, doubling and redoubling into braids and garlands, lustrous, self-satisfied. They were long enough now to brush with her fingertips, then to drape around her shoulders, necklaces, scarves. They had the seamlessness of the fur of a healthy animal; she learned to trust in their cohesion, their tensile strength. She knew herself, still, to be a creature bounded by gravity, but now she could travel from room to room never touching the floor. She sensed his approaching footsteps not as sound nor even as vibration but only as a stirring among the coils at her throat.

MARI Y JUANA
~ translated by Steven Bradbury

Lyricism's a fait accompli
We can now remain aloof from
All that's left is action
We must become involved

I really do love you even more than before
On top of which I want to forget you even less
As always I'm ready to go crazy over you
As always the thought of you can make me blue

By the pawnshop is a Tu Di Gong (tutelary god of wealth and well-being)
Where anything is pawnable for to ask is to receive
In dribs and drabs we fritter away our lives every evening

Either I could use another toke or you're still too sober
Of course it could be the poetry is lousy
Or else this town is way off key

MARI Y JUANA
~ Original by Hsia Yü 夏宇

抒情已經完成
可以置身事外
剩下的是動作
用來置身事內

我「的比從前更愛「
更加不要把「忘記
我依然隨時可以「「瘋狂
我依然隨時可以「「受傷

當鋪旁邊是土地公
萬物可當有求必應
「上我們也要一起「一些鳥事浪費我們的生命

不是我抽得不「就是「們還太「醒
當然也可能是詩太爛
否則就是這個城市根本不配

Contributors' Biographies

Shamshad Abdullaev (b. 1957) is the former, and last, poetry editor of *Zvezda Vostoka* (Tashkent, Uzbekistan), which was shut down in 1994. He has been awarded the Adrey Bely prize (1993), the Znamya prize (1998,) and the Russia/Yeltsin prize (2006; also short-listed this year.) The Russian originals may be found on Vavilon.ru. Abdullaev's other poems, in Alex's English translation, are in *Modern Poetry in Translation, Literary Imagination, The Manhattan Review, St. Petersburg Review*, and *Two Lines* (translated by Valzyna Mort). He is the author of two books of prose and three of poems, the latest being *Approaching Periphery; Poems and Essays* (NLO, 2013).

Kim Addonizio's latest books are *My Black Angel: Blues Poems and Portraits*, with woodcuts by Charles D. Jones, and *Lucifer at the Starlite*. Her honors include a Guggenheim Fellowship, two NEA Fellowships, and Pushcart Prizes for both poetry and the essay. Her collection *Tell Me* was a National Book Award Finalist. Other books include two novels from Simon & Schuster, *Little Beauties* and *My Dreams Out in the Street*. Her new story collection, *The Palace of Illusions*, materialized courtesy of Counterpoint/Soft Skull in September 2014. Addonizio offers private poetry workshops in Oakland, NYC, and online, and often incorporates her love of blues harmonica into her readings. kimaddonizio.com.

Kelli Russell Agodon is an award-winning poet, writer, and editor from the Pacific Northwest. Her most recent collection is *Hourglass Museum* (White Pine Press, 2014) and *The Daily Poet: Day-By-Day Prompts for Your Writing Practice*, which she coauthored with Martha Silano. Her second collection, *Letters from the Emily Dickinson Room*, was chosen by Carl Dennis as the winner of the White Pine Press Book Prize, and was also the Winner of *ForeWord Magazine*'s Book of the Year in Poetry as well as a Finalist for the Washington State Book Prize. Her other books include *Small Knots, Geography*, and *Fire*

On Her Tongue: An Anthology of Contemporary Women's Poetry. Kelli is the cofounder of Two Sylvias Press and is a Co-Director of Poets on the Coast: A Retreat for Women Poets. She lives in a small seaside town where she is an avid paddleboarder, mountain biker, and hiker who has a fondness for writing letters, desserts, and fedoras. agodon.com

Sandra Alcosser's books of poetry, which include *A Fish to Feed All Hunger* and *Except by Nature*, have been selected for the National Poetry Series, the Academy of American Poets James Laughlin Award, the Larry Levis Award, the Associated Writing Programs Award in Poetry, and the William Stafford Award from Pacific Northwest Booksellers. She was National Endowment for the Arts' first Conservation Poet for the Wildlife Conservation Society and Poets House, New York, as well as Montana's first poet laureate and recipient of the Merriam Award for Distinguished Contribution to Montana Literature. She founded and directs SDSU's MFA each fall and serves on the graduate faculty of Pacific University. She received two individual artist fellowships from NEA, and her poems have appeared in the *New York Times, The New Yorker, The Paris Review, Poetry* and the *Pushcart Prize Anthology.*

Meena Alexander's eighth book of poetry, *Atmospheric Embroidery*, is forthcoming in June 2015 from Hachette India. Her works include the book of essays *Poetics of Dislocation* (University of Michigan Press, Poets on Poetry Series, 2009) and the critically acclaimed memoir *Fault Lines.* She is Distinguished Professor of English, Graduate Center/Hunter College, CUNY. meenaalexander.com

Kazim Ali ('98): his books of poetry include *The Far Mosque, The Fortieth Day*, the cross-genre memoir *Bright Felon: Autobiography and Cities*, and most recently, *Sky Ward.* He is also the author of two novels, *Quinn's Passage* and *The Disappearance of Seth* and the essay collections *Orange Alert: Essays on Poetry, Art and the Architecture of Silence* and *Fasting for Ramadan: Notes from a Spiritual Practice.* He has translated volumes by Marguerite Duras, Sohrab Sepehri and Ananda Devi. In addition to his work as a yoga teacher and political organizer,

Kazim teaches at Oberlin College and has served as visiting faculty in various low-residency MFA programs including New England College, Naropa University, Stonecoast, Antioch University and Murray State University. Kazim co-founded Nightboat Books in 2004 with fellow Squaw Valley alum Jennifer Chapis.

Ralph Angel's *Your Moon* received the 2013 Green Rose Poetry Prize, and is available from New Issues. His *Exceptions and Melancholies: Poems 1986–2006* received the 2007 PEN USA Poetry Award, and *Neither World* won the James Laughlin Award of the Academy of American Poets. In addition to five books of poetry, he has also published an award-winning translation of the Federico García Lorca collection *Poema del cante jondo / Poem of the Deep Song*.

Rae Armantrout's new book, *Itself*, was published by Wesleyan in February 2015. She has published eleven books of poetry and has also been featured in a number of major anthologies. Her book of poems *Versed* was awarded the 2009 National Book Critics Circle Award and the 2010 Pulitzer Prize for Poetry. Armantrout's most recent collection is *Just Saying*.

David Baker's sixteen books include *Scavenger Loop* (W. W. Norton, poems, 2015), *Show Me Your Environment: Essays on Poetry, Poets, and Poems* (University of Michigan, 2014), and *Never-Ending Birds* (W. W. Norton, poems) which was awarded the Theodore Roethke Memorial Poetry Prize in 2011. He lives in rural Ohio and is Poetry Editor of *The Kenyon Review*.

Sally Ball is the author of *Wreck Me* (Barrow Street, 2013) and *Annus Mirabilis*, which was selected by Ellen Bryant Voigt for the Barrow Street Press Poetry Prize (Barrow Street, 2005). She is an associate director of Four Way Books.

Benno Barnard has published a considerable body of poetry and prose, including *Krijg nou de lyriek* (*Get Lyricked!*, 2011) and *Een vage* *buitenlander* (*A Vague Foreigner*, 2009). He has been awarded several prestigious prizes. Eyewear Publishing in London are planning a selection of his poetry in 2015, *A Public Woman: Selected Poems*.

Ciaran Berry is a 2012 Whiting Writers' Award winner. His full-length collections are *The Sphere of Birds* (2008) and *The Dead Zoo* (2013), which was a recent Poetry Book Society Recommendation. Originally from the west of Ireland, he directs the creative writing program at Trinity College in Hartford, Connecticut, where he lives with his wife and two sons.

Linda Bierds' most recent book, *Roget's Illusion*, was longlisted for the 2014 National Book Award. Her awards include fellowships from the Guggenheim and MacArthur foundations and twice from the NEA. She teaches at the University of Washington in Seattle.

Sally Bliumis-Dunn teaches Modern Poetry at Manhattanville College. She recieved her MFA in Poetry from Sarah Lawrence in 2002. Her poems have appeared in *Bellevue Literary Review, From the Fishouse, The Paris Review, PBS NewsHour, Prairie Schooner, PLUME, Poetry London*, the *New York Times,* Terrain.org, *The Writer's Almanac* and The Academy of American Poets' Poem-a-day series, among others. In 2002, she was a finalist for the Nimrod/Hardman Pablo Neruda Prize. Her two books, *Talking Underwater* and *Second Skin*, were published by Wind Publications in 2007 and 2009, respectively.

Stephen Todd Booker, born in 1953, is originally from Brooklyn, and has spent 38 years in prison, 34 on Death Row in Florida, where he started writing poetry. His work has appeared in numerous publications worldwide, most recently in *the new renaissance, Mudlark*, and *Watershed*. He's the author of three collections: *Waves and License* (Greenfield Review Press); *Tug* (Wesleyan U. Press); & *Swiftly, Deeper* (Mandrake Poetry Press)

David Bottoms' first book, *Shooting Rats at the Bibb County Dump* (William Morrow, 1980), was chosen by Robert Penn Warren as winner of the 1979 Walt Whitman Award of the Academy of American Poets. His poems have appeared widely in magazines such as *The Atlantic, The New Yorker, Harper's, Poetry,* and *The Paris Review,* as well as in sixty anthologies and textbooks. He is the author of seven other books of poetry, two novels, and a book of essays and interviews. His most recent book of poems is *We Almost Disappear* (Copper Canyon Press, 2011).

Daniel Bourne's books of poetry include *The Household Gods* (Cleveland State University Press, 1995), *Where No One Spoke the Language* (CustomWords, 2006) and a collection of translations of the Polish political poet Tomasz Jastrun, *On the Crossroads of Asia and Europe* (Salmon Run, 1999). He teaches in the English Department and Environmental Studies at the College of Wooster, where he edits *Artful Dodge.* His many trips to Poland include a graduate fellowship between Indiana University and Warsaw University in 1982–83 and a Fulbright fellowship in 1985–87 for the translation of younger Polish poets. His poems have appeared in such journals as *Plume, Ploughshares, FIELD, Guernica, American Poetry Review, Prairie Schooner, Shenandoah, Salmagundi, Tar River Poetry,* and *Cimarron Review.* His translations of other Polish poets such as Bronisław Maj and Zbigniew Machej appear in *FIELD, Boulevard, Mid-American Review, Virginia Quarterly Review,* and elsewhere. In July 2013, *Plume* printed as its Special Feature his translations of another Polish poet, "The Angel's Share: Six Poems by Krzysztof Kuczkowski." Finally, "Agitprop" and "To the Feral Cats of Vilnius," two of Bourne's poems from his collection *Where No One Spoke the Language* and originally appearing in *Salmagundi,* will be re-printed in a special issue celebrating that journal's 50th anniversary in the coming year.

Steve Bradbury's translation of Hsia Yü's *Salsa* collection was recently published by Zephyr Press. He lives in northern Florida near the Ichetucknee Springs.

Christopher Buckley's 20th poetry book is *Back Room at the Philosophers' Club* (Stephen F. Austin State Univ. Press, 2014). *Varieties of Religious Experience* (SFA, 2013). Third nonfiction book, *Holy Days of Obligation* (Lynx House Press, 2014). Editor *On The Poetry of Philip Levine: Stranger to Nothing*. Recipient of a Guggenheim in Poetry, two NEAs, Fulbright Award in Creative Writing, four Pushcart Prizes; 2013 winner of the Campbell Corner Poetry Contest.

Michael Burkard's most recent book is *lucky coat anywhere* (nightboat books). Two books of drawings and writings are available from blurb. com, *one day my face* and *a flower with milk in a shadow beside it*.

Although he was admired by leading poets of the Italian "hermetic" movement, **Lorenzo Calogero** (1910–1961) has long remained a major overlooked figure in Italian poetry. His collected poems were first gathered in a two-volume *Opere Poetiche* (Lerici Editori, 1962 / 1966) and in a representative selection, *Poesie* (Rubbettino Editore, 1986). Recently, new editions of his work have appeared, notably *Avaro nel tuo pensiero* (Donzelli, 2014), *Poco Suono* (Nuove Edizioni Barbaro, 2011) and especially *Parole del tempo* (Donzelli, 2010). A revival of interest in his work is definitely underway. He sporadically worked as a medical doctor, spent time confined to mental asylums, and seems to have committed suicide in his house in Meliccucà (Calabria), but the circumstances of his death were never entirely clarified. The poems presented here have been selected from the posthumously published manuscript *Come in dittici* (*As in Diptychs*), included in the first volume of the *Opere Poetiche*.

Peter Campion is the author of three collections of poems, *Other People* (2005), *The Lions* (2009), and *El Dorado* (2013). He teaches in the MFA program in creative writing at the University of Minnesota.

José Manuel Cardona is a poet from Ibiza, Spain. He is the author of *El Vendimiador* (Atzavara, 1953); *Poemas a Circe* (Adonais, 1959); and the anthology *The Birnam Wood* (Consell Insular d'Eivissa, 2007), published by the government of Ibiza. He was co-editor of several literary journals and wrote for many publications. He participated in the II Congreso de Poesía in Salamanca and wrote his thesis on the Mexican revolution at the Instituto de Cultura Hispánica de Madrid. The Franco regime forced him into exile in France. He is an attorney (University of Barcelona) and holds PhDs in Literature and Humanities (University of Nancy), and Political Sciences and Economy (IHEI, Geneva). He worked for the UN most of his life, in Geneva, Paris, Rome, Vienna, Belgrade, Sofia, Kiev, Tblisi, Moscow, St. Petersburg, and Panama, among many places.

Hélène Cardona is a poet, linguist, dream analyst, author of *Dreaming My Animal Selves* (Salmon Poetry), winner of the Pinnacle Book Award and the 2014 Readers' Favorite Award in *Poetry; The Astonished Universe* (Red Hen Press); and *Life in Suspension*, forthcoming from Salmon Poetry in 2016. *Ce que nous portons* (Éditions du Cygne, 2014) is her translation of *What We Carry* by Dorianne Laux. She also translated *Beyond Elsewhere* by Gabriel Arnou-Laujeac. She holds a Masters in English & American Literature from the Sorbonne, taught at Hamilton College & Loyola Marymount University, and received fellowships from the Goethe-Institut & Universidad Internacional de Andalucía. She is co-editor of *Dublin Poetry Review* and *Levure Littéraire*. Other publications include *Washington Square, World Literature Today, Poetry International, The Warwick Review, The Dublin Review of Books, The Irish Literary Times, The Los Angeles Review*, and many more.

Alex Cigale's own English-language poems have appeared in *Colorado, Green Mountains, North American, Tampa*, and *The Literary Reviews*, and online in *Drunken Boat* and *McSweeney's*. His translations from Russian can be found in *Beloit Poetry Journal, Cimarron Review, Literary Imagination, Modern Poetry in Translation, New England Review, PEN America, Two Lines*, and *World Literature Today*. From 2011 until 2013, Alex was an Assistant Professor at the American University of Central Asia in Bishkek, Kyrgyzstan. He was recently awarded the 2015 NEA Literary Translation Fellowship for his work on the poet of the St. Petersburg philological school, Mikhail Eremin.

Andrea Cohen's poems have appeared in *The New Yorker*, *The Atlantic Monthly*, *Poetry*, *The Threepenny Review*, and elsewhere. Her new collection, *Furs Not Mine*, is forthcoming from Four Way Books. She directs the Blacksmith House Poetry Series in Cambridge, Massachusetts and the Writers House at Merrimack College.

Michael Collier, director of the Bread Loaf Writers' Conference, has published six books of poems, including *The Ledge*, a finalist for the National Book Critics Circle Award and the *Los Angeles Times* Book Prize, and, most recently, *An Individual History*. With Charles Baxter and Edward Hirsch, he edited *A William Maxwell Portrait*. He has received an Award in Literature from the American Academy of Arts and Letters, Guggenheim Foundation and Thomas Watson Foundation fellowships, and two National Endowment for the Arts fellowships. Poet Laureate of Maryland 2001–2004, he teaches in the creative writing program at the University of Maryland.

Billy Collins' latest collection is *Aimless Love: New and Selected Poems* (Random House, 2013). He is a Distinguished Professor at Lehman College (CUNY) and a Senior Distinguished Fellow of the Winter Park Institute at Rollins College. He served as United States Poet Laureate (2001–2003).

Martha Collins' eighth book of poems, *Admit One: An American Scrapbook*, will be published by Pittsburgh in early 2016. Collins is also the author of seven earlier books of poetry, most recently *Day Unto Day*, *White Papers*, and *Blue Front*, and co-translator of four collections of Vietnamese poetry. She is editor-at-large for *FIELD* magazine and an editor for the Oberlin College Press.

David Colmer is an Australian translator, mainly of Dutch-language literature, and the winner of numerous translation awards. Recent books include collections of the poetry of Hugo Claus and Cees Nooteboom. His translation of a selection of Benno Bernard's poetry, *A Public Woman*, will be published by Eyewear Publishing in 2015.

Peter Cooley's latest book of poetry is *Night Bus to the Afterlife*. Recent poems have appeared in *The Southern Review, The Hopkins Review, The Other Journal*, and *Conte*. He is Senior Mellon Professor in the Humanities at Tulane and Director of Creative Writing, and the Poetry Editor of *Christianity and Literature*.

Steven Cramer is the author of five poetry collections: *The Eye that Desires to Look Upward* (1987), *The World Book* (1992), *Dialogue for the Left and Right Hand* (1997), *Goodbye to the Orchard* (Sarabande, 2004)—which won the 2005 Sheila Motton Prize from the New England Poetry Club and was a 2005 Honor Book in Poetry by the Massachusetts Center for the Book—and *Clangings* (Sarabande, 2012). He directs the MFA Program in Creative Writing at Lesley University.

Cynthia Cruz's poems have been published in *The New Yorker, The Paris Review, Boston Review, American Poetry Review, Kenyon Review*, and others. Her first collection of poems, *RUIN*, was published by Alice James Books, her second and third collections, *The Glimmering Room* and *Wunderkammer*, were published by Four Way Books. She has received fellowships from Yaddo and the MacDowell Colony as well as a Hodder Fellowship fromPrinceton University. She teaches at Sarah Lawrence College and lives in Brooklyn,New York.

Lydia Davis' most recent book is *Can't and Won't*, from FSG, 2014.

Ghanaian-born Jamaican poet **Kwame Dawes** is the award-winning author of sixteen books of poetry (including, *Wheels*, 2011) and numerous books of fiction, non-fiction, criticism and drama. He is the Glenna Luschei Editor of *Prairie Schooner*, and a Chancellor's Professor of English at the University of Nebraska. Kwame Dawes also teaches in the Pacific MFA Writing program. Dawes' book, *Duppy Conqueror: New and Selected Poems* was published by Copper Canyon in 2013.

Norman Dubie's most recent collection of poems, *The Quotations of Bone*, will be published by Copper Canyon Press in spring 2015.

Stephen Dunn is the author of seventeen collections of poetry, including the *Here and Now* and *What Goes On: Selected & New Poems 1995–2009*. *Different Hours* won the Pulitzer Prize in 2001, and *Loosestrife* was a National Book Critics Circle Award finalist in 1996. His most recent collection is *Lines of Defense* (Norton, 2014). This poem is part of a chapbook-length sequence called *Seeker of Limits: The Cavendish Poems*, forthcoming from Sarabande in September 2015.

Lynn Emanuel is the author of four books of poetry, *Hotel Fiesta, The Dig, Then, Suddenly*—, and, most recently, *Noose and Hook*. A volume of her new and selected poetry, *The Nerve Of It*, will be forthcoming in the fall of 2015. Her work has been featured in the *Pushcart Prize Anthology* and *Best American Poetry* numerous times and is included in *The Oxford Book of American Poetry*. She has been a judge for the National Book Awards and has taught at the Bread Loaf Writers' Conference, The Warren Wilson Program in Creative Writing, and the Bennington College Low Residency MFA program. She is the recipient of two fellowships from the National Endowment for the Arts, The National Poetry Series Award, the Eric Matthieu King Award from The Academy of American Poets and, most recently, a fellowship from the Ranieri Foundation.

Sylva Fischerová was born in 1963 in Prague. She grew up in the Moravian town of Olomouc as a daughter of non-Marxist philosopher whose works were banished under communist rule. She returned to Prague to study philosophy and physics, and later Greek and Latin, at Charles University where she now teaches ancient Greek literature and philosophy. She has published six volumes of poems in Czech, and her poetry has been translated and published in numerous languages. An earlier selection of her poems, *The Tremor of Racehorses*, translated by Ian and Jarmila Milner, was published by Bloodaxe in 1990. She recently began to write prose, and a book of her stories, *Miracle*, as well as a book for children, appeared in 2005. *The Swing in the Middle of Chaos: Selected Poems*, co-translated with Stuart Friebert, was published by Bloodaxe in 2009.

Luigi Fontanella is the editor of *Gradiva* and the president of IPA (Italian Poetry in America). His most recent books of poetry are *Bertgang* (Moretti & Vitali, 2012, Prata Prize, I Murazzi Prize) and *Disunita Ombra* (Archinto-Rizzoli, 2013, Frascati Prize). He lives in Florence, Italy, and Long Island, NY. Luigi. Fontanella@stonybrook.edu

Allen Forrest was born in Canada and bred in the U.S. He works in many mediums: oil painting, computer graphics, theatre, digital music, film, and video. Allen studied acting at Columbia Pictures in Los Angeles, digital media in art and design at Bellevue College (receiving degrees in Web Multimedia Authoring and Digital Video Production.) He works in Vancouver, BC, as a graphic artist and painter. Forrest's expressive drawing and painting style creates emotion on canvas.

Stuart Friebert has published thirteen books of poems, including *Funeral Pie*, co-winner of the Four Way Book Award. A 14th, *On the Bottom*, will appear soon from Iris Press. In addition, he's published ten volumes of translations, most recently *Puppets in the Wind: Selected Poems of Karl Krolow* (Bitter Oleander Press); and an eleventh will soon appear from Tiger Bark Press: *Be Quiet: Selected Poems of Kuno Raeber*, as will a collection of memoir pieces and stories, *The Language of the Enemy* (Black Mountain Press. With David Young, he's co-edited *The Longman Anthology of Contemporary American Poetry* (2 editions.); and *Models of the Universe*, an anthology of prose poems.

Philip Fried has published six books of poetry. His most recent collection is *Interrogating Water* (Salmon, 2014), which Carol Rumens, writing in *The Guardian*, praised for "the valor and vision of its protest." He has recently published work in *Poetry*, the *Notre Dame Review*, *Poetry Review*, and *Poet Lore*, and is preparing a manuscript titled *Squaring the Circle*. In addition to writing poems, he is the founding editor of *The Manhattan Review*.

Jeff Friedman's sixth collection of poetry, *Pretenders*, was published by Carnegie Mellon University Press in 2014. His poems, mini-stories and translations have appeared in many literary magazines, including *American Poetry Review, Poetry, New England Review, The Antioch Review, Poetry International, Hotel Amerika, Vestal Review, Quick Fiction, Flash Fiction Funny, Smokelong Quarterly, Prairie Schooner, 100-Word Story, Plume, Solstice*, and *The New Republic*. Dzvinia Orlowsky's and his translation of *Memorials* by Polish poet Mieczslaw Jastrun was published by Lavender Ink/Dialogos in 2014. A contributing editor to *Natural Bridge* and *Anthem Literary Journal*, he lives in West Lebanon, New Hampshire with the artist Colleen Randall and their dog Ruby.

Four Pushcart Prize anthologies have published poems by **Carol Frost**, as well as *Poetry, The New Republic, Gettysburg Review, The Atlantic, the New York Times, Subtropics*, and *The Kenyon Review*. *Entwined: Three Lyric Sequences*, her twelfth collection, appeared this fall from Tupelo Press. She teaches at Rollins College, where she is the Theodore Bruce and Barbara Lawrence Alfond Professor of English and she directs Winter with the Writers, a yearly literary festival.

Forrest Gander's most recent books are *The Trace*, a novel; *Eiko & Koma*, a book of poetry and collaboration with the eponymous movement artists, and *Fungus Skull Eye Wing*, translations of the selected poems of Mexican poet Alfonso D'Aquino.

Amy Gerstler's most recent books of poetry include *Dearest Creature, Ghost Girl, Medicine*, and *Crown of Weeds*. Her book of poems *Bitter Angel* received a National Book Critics' Circle Award in 1991. Her work has appeared in numerous magazines and anthologies, including *The New Yorker, Poetry, The Paris Review, American Poetry Review*, several volumes of *Best American Poetry*, and the *Norton Anthology of Postmodern American Poetry*. She teaches at University of California at Irvine.

Ani Gjika was born and raised in Albania and moved to the U.S. at age 18. She is a 2010 Robert Pinsky Global Fellow and winner of a 2010 Robert Fitzgerald Translation Prize. Her first book, *Bread on Running*

Waters, (Fenway Press, 2013) was a finalist for the 2011 Anthony Hecht Poetry Prize, 2011 May Sarton New Hampshire Book Prize, and 2011 Crab Orchard Series Award. Poems and translations have appeared or are forthcoming in *Ploughshares, AGNI Online, Salamander, Seneca Review, World Literature Today, Two Lines Online, From the Fishouse*, and elsewhere.

Douglas Goetsch has published several volumes of poems, most recently *Nameless Boy* (2015, Orchises Press). His work has appeared in *The New Yorker, Poetry, The Gettysburg Review, The American Scholar, Best American Poetry*, and the *Pushcart Prize Anthology*. His honors include fellowships from the National Endowment for the Arts, the New York Foundation for the Arts, and the Donald Murray Prize. He is founding editor of Jane Street Press, and teaches writing in private workshops and online. douglasgoetsch.com.

Beckian Fritz Goldberg received her MFA in 1985 from Vermont College and is the author of seven volumes of poetry, *Body Betrayer* (Cleveland State University Press, 1991,) *In the Badlands of Desire* (Cleveland State University, 1993,) *Never Be the Horse*, winner of the University of Akron Poetry Prize (University of Akron Press, 1999), *Twentieth Century Children*, a limited-edition chapbook, winner of the *Indiana Review* chapbook prize (Graphic Design Press, Indiana University, 1999), *Lie Awake Lake*, winner of the 2004 *Field* Poetry Prize (Oberlin College Press, 2005) *The Book of Accident* (University of Akron Press, 2006,) *Reliquary Fever: New and Selected Poems* (New Issues Press, 2010) and *Egypt From Space* (Oberlin, 2013.) Goldberg has been awarded the Theodore Roethke Poetry Prize from *Poetry Northwest, The Gettysburg Review* Annual Poetry Prize, two Arizona Commission on the Arts Poetry Fellowships (1993, 2001) and two Pushcart Prizes. Her work has appeared in numerous anthologies such as *New American Poets of the 90s, Best American Poetry 1995, American Alphabets: 25 Contemporary Poets, Best American Poetry 2011, Best American Poetry 2013*, and in journals, including *The American Poetry Review, Field, The Gettysburg Review, Harper's, The Iowa Review*,

Michigan Quarterly Review, Gulf Coast, and many others. She currently lives in Arizona.

Arielle Greenberg's new poetry collection, *Slice,* just came out, and her creative nonfiction book *Locally Made Panties* is forthcoming in 2016. She's also the author of the previous poetry books *My Kafka Century* and *Given,* and the chapbooks *Shake Her* and *Fa(r)ther Down: Songs from the Allergy Trials.* She is co-author, with Rachel Zucker, of *Home/ Birth: A Poemic,* and co-editor of three anthologies: most recently, with Lara Glenum, *Gurlesque.* Her poems and essays have been featured in anthologies including *Best American Poetry, Labor Day: True Birth Stories for the 21st Century* and *The Arcadia Project: North American Postmodern Pastoral,* and she writes a regular column on contemporary poetics for the *American Poetry Review.* A former tenured professor in poetry at Columbia College Chicago, she now lives in Maine and teaches in the community and in Oregon State University–Cascades' MFA.

Jeffrey Greene is AUP's Creative Writing Coordinator. He is the author of four collections of poetry, a memoir, and two nature books. His most recent book is *Shades of the Other Shore,* Cahier Series 20, a multi-genre exploration with artist and AUP professor Ralph Petty. His new book on the cult of wild edibles is forthcoming in 2015.

Kelle Groom's poetry collections are *Five Kingdoms, Luckily* (both from Anhinga), and *Underwater City* (University Press of Florida). Her memoir, *I Wore the Ocean in the Shape of a Girl* (Simon & Schuster), is a Barnes & Noble Discover Great New Writers selection, *New York Times* Book Review Editor's Choice, and a *Library Journal* Best Memoir. Her work appears in *Agni, The New Yorker, New York Times, Ploughshares, Poetry,* and *Best American Poetry.* A 2014 NEA Literature Fellow, she is also the recipient of fellowships and awards from Black Mountain Institute, University of Nevada–Las Vegas, Library of Congress, and James Merrill House, among others. Recently Distinguished Writer-in-Residence at Sierra Nevada College, Lake Tahoe, Groom is now on the faculty of SNC's low-residency MFA Program. She is at work on a second memoir. This poem is from the manuscript of her fourth poetry collection, *SPILL*.

Rachel Hadas has two new books forthcoming: *Talking to the Dead* (Spuyten Duyvil Press, 2015) and *Questions in the Vestibule* (Northwestern Univ. Press, 2016). Her poems appear regularly in *The New Yorker*.

Kimiko Hahn is the author of nine collections and often finds that disparate sources have triggered her material—whether Flaubert's sex-tour in *The Unbearable Heart*, an exhumation in *The Artist's Daughter*, or classical Japanese forms in *The Narrow Road to the Interior*. Rarefied fields of science prompted her latest collections *Toxic Flora* and *Brain Fever* (both W.W. Norton) as well as a new chapbook, *Cryptic Chamber* (Epiphany). Collaborations have led her to film and the visual arts. Hahn's most recent award was a Guggenheim Fellowship; she is a distinguished professor in the MFA Program in Creative Writing & Literary Translation at Queens College, The City University of New York.

Barbara Hamby's book of stories, *Lester Higata's 20th Century*, won the Iowa Short Fiction Prize/John Simmons Award, she was named a Distinguished University Scholar at Florida State, and she received a Guggenheim Fellowship. She also published *Seriously Funny*, an anthology of poetry that she co-edited with her husband David Kirby, and Amy Gerstler chose five of her Lingo Sonnets for *Best American Poetry 2010*.

Bob Hicok's latest book, *Elegy Owed* (Copper Canyon, 2013), was a finalist for the National Book Critics Circle Award. *Sex & Love &* will be published by Copper Canyon in 2016.

Brenda Hillman has published chapbooks with Penumbra Press, a+bend press, and EmPress; she is the author of nine full-length collections from Wesleyan University Press, the most recent of which are *Practical Water* (2009) and *Seasonal Works with Letters on Fire* (2013). With Patricia Dienstfrey, she edited *The Grand Permission: New Writings on Poetics and Motherhood* (Wesleyan, 2003). Hillman teaches at St. Mary's College of California where she is the Olivia C. Filippi Professor of Poetry; she is an activist for social and environmental justice and lives in the San Francisco Bay Area. blueflowerarts.com/brenda-hillman/ amd brendahillman.net/bio.html

Jane Hirshfield's eighth poetry collection, *The Beauty*, appeared from Knopf in March 2015, along with a new book of essays, *Ten Windows*. Previous books include *Come, Thief* (2011); and *After* (2006), named a best book of the year by *The Washington Post*, *The San Francisco Chronicle*, and England's *Financial Times*. Her work has appeared in *The New Yorker*, *The Atlantic*, *Harper's*, *Poetry*, *McSweeney's*, *Orion*, and eight editions of *Best American Poetry*. Her honors include fellowships from the NEA, the Guggenheim and Rockefeller foundations, and the Academy of American Poets, as well as the California Book Award, The Poetry Center Book Award, and finalist selection for the National Book Critics Circle Award. In 2012, she was named the third recipient of the Donald Hall–Jane Kenyon Prize in American Poetry and elected a chancellor of the Academy of American Poets..

Tony Hoagland's books of poetry include *Sweet Ruin* (1992), which was chosen for the Brittingham Prize in Poetry; *Donkey Gospel* (1998), winner of the James Laughlin Award; *What Narcissism Means to Me* (2003), a finalist for the National Book Critics Circle Award. A new collection of poems is due from Graywolf in September 2015.

Jay Hopler's poetry, essays, and translations have appeared most recently or are forthcoming in *The Literary Review*, *The New Republic*, and *The New Yorker*. *Green Squall*, his first book of poetry, won the 2005 Yale Series of Younger Poets Award. His most recent book is *Before the Door of God: An Anthology of Devotional Poetry* (edited with Kimberly Johnson, Yale University Press, 2013). The recipient of numerous honors including fellowships and awards from the Great

Lakes Colleges Association, the Lannan Foundation, the Mrs. Giles Whiting Foundation, and the American Academy of Arts & Letters/ the American Academy in Rome, he is Associate Professor of English at the University of South Florida.

Recipient of the Richard Wright Prize for Literature and a Guggenheim Fellowship in Poetry, **T. R. Hummer** is an internationally recognized poet and scholar who was born and raised in Macon, Mississippi. His new book of poems, *Ephemeron*, was published by LSU Press in 2011, and a new book of essays, *Available Surfaces*, appeared in the University of Michigan Press's "Poets on Poetry" series in 2012.

Mark Irwin's seventh collection of poetry, *Large White House Speaking*, appeared from *New Issues* in spring of 2013, and his *American Urn: New & Selected Poems (1987–2014)* will be published in 2015. Recognition for his work includes The Nation / Discovery Award, two Colorado Book Awards, four Pushcart Prizes, and fellowships from the Fulbright, Lilly, NEA, and Wurlitzer Foundations. He teaches in the Ph.D. in Creative Writing & Literature Program at the University of Southern California and he lives in Los Angeles and Colorado.

Devin Johnston is the author of five books of poetry, including *Far-Fetched* (FSG, 2015). He works for Flood Editions, a nonprofit publishing house, and teaches at Saint Louis University.

Marilyn Kallet is the author of 16 books including *The Love That Moves Me*, poetry by Black Widow Press, 2013. She has also translated Paul Eluard's *Last Love Poems* (*Derniers poèmes d'amour*) and Benjamin Péret's *The Big Game* (Le grand jeu). Kallet directs the Creative Writing Program at the University of Tennessee, where she is Nancy Moore Goslee Professor of English. Each spring she leads poetry workshops for the Virginia Center for the Creative Arts in Auvillar, France

Laura Kasischke is the recipient of the National Book Critics Circle Award for Poetry, 2012. She has published eight novels, two of which have been made into feature films—*The Life Before Her Eyes* and *Suspicious River*—and eight books of poetry. She has received fellowships from the Guggenheim Foundation, the National Endowment for the Arts, as well as several Pushcart Prizes and numerous poetry awards. Her writing has appeared in *Best American Poetry, The Kenyon Review, Harper's,* and *The New Republic.* She lives with her family in Chelsea, Michigan and is an Allan Seager Collegiate Professor of English Language and Literature at the University of Michigan.

Dore Kiesselbach's *Salt Pier* (Pittsburgh, 2012) won the Agnes Lynch Starrett Prize and features work selected for Britain's Bridport Prize and the Poetry Society of America's Robert H. Winner Memorial Award. A 2015 Minnesota State Arts Board grant recipient and former U.S. Department of Education Jacob K. Javits Fellow, he has published in *Agni, Field, Plume, Poetry, Stand,* and other leading magazines.

John Kinsella is founding editor of the journal *Salt* in Australia; he serves as international editor at the *Kenyon Review.* His most recent volumes of poetry are *Divine Comedy: Journeys through a Regional Geography* (W. W. Norton, 2010) and *Jam Tree Gully* (W. W. Norton, 2011).

David Kirby is the author of more than two dozen volumes of criticism, essays, children's literature, pedagogy, and poetry. His numerous collections of poetry include *The Ha-Ha* (2003), short-listed for the Griffin Poetry Prize, and *The House on Boulevard Street: New and Selected Poems* (2007), a finalist for the National Book Award and winner of the Florida Book Award and the Southern Independent Booksellers Alliance Award

Karl Kirchwey is the author of six books of poems, most recently *Mount Lebanon* (Marian Wood/Putnam, 2011), as well as a translation of Paul Verlaine's first book, titled *Poems Under Saturn* (Princeton University Press, 2011). His new manuscript is *Stumbling Blocks: Roman Poems.* Kirchwey is currently Professor of English and Director of Creative

Writing at Boston University, and from 2010 to 2013 served as Andrew Heiskell Arts Director at the American Academy in Rome.

Jennifer L. Knox's new book of poems, *Days of Shame and Failure*, will be published by Bloof Books in October 2015. Her poems have appeared four times in *Best American Poetry* as well as *The New Yorker, American Poetry Review, McSweeney's*, and *Bomb*. She teaches at Iowa State University.

Yusef Komunyakaa's books of poetry include *Taboo, Dien Cai Dau, Neon Vernacular*, for which he received the Pulitzer Prize, *Warhorses, The Chameleon Couch* and, most recently, *Testimony*. His plays, performance art and libretti have been performed internationally and include *Saturnalia, Testimony*, and *Gilgamesh*. He teaches at New York University.

Dorianne Laux's most recent books of poems are *The Book of Men*, winner of the Paterson Poetry Prize, and *Facts about the Moon*, recipient of the Oregon Book Award and short-listed for the Lenore Marshall Poetry Prize. Laux is also author of *Awake, What We Carry*, finalist for the National Book Critic's Circle Award, and *Smoke*. In 2014 singer/songwriter Joan Osborne adapted her poem, "The Shipfitter's Wife" and set it to music on her newest release, *Love and Hate*. She teaches poetry and directs the MFA program at North Carolina State University and she is founding faculty at Pacific University's Low Residency MFA Program.

Hank Lazer's eighteen books of poetry include *N24* (hand-sewn, handwritten chapbook in the Little Red Leaves Textile Series), *N18* (complete) from Singing Horse Press (2012), *Portions* (Lavender Ink, 2009), *The New Spirit* (Singing Horse, 2005), *Elegies & Vacations* (Salt, 2004), and *Days* (Lavender Ink, 2002). In 2008, *Lyric & Spirit: Selected Essays, 1996–2008* was published by Omnidawn. Pages from the notebooks have been performed with soprano saxophonist Andrew

Raffo Dewar at the University of Georgia and in Havana, Cuba. Features on the Notebooks appear in *Talisman* 42 and *Plume* 34.

Sydney Lea's most recent poetry book is *Young of the Year* (Four Way Books, 2011.) A twelfth collection, *No Doubt the Nameless*, is due in 2016 from Four Way Books His stories, poems, essays and criticism have appeared in *The New Yorker, The Atlantic, The New Republic, The New York Times, Sports Illustrated, Gray's Sporting Journal*, and many other periodicals, as well as in more than forty anthologies. He is the Poet Laureate of Vermont

Phillis Levin's fifth collection, *Mr. Memory & Other Poems*, will be published by Penguin in April 2016. She is the author of four other collections, *Temples and Fields* (University of Georgia Press, 1988), *The Afterimage* (Copper Beech Press, 1995), *Mercury* (Penguin, 2001), and *May Day* (Penguin, 2008), and is editor of *The Penguin Book of the Sonnet* (2001). Her honors include the Poetry Society of America's Norma Farber First Book Award, a Fulbright Scholar Award to Slovenia, the Amy Lowell Poetry Travelling Scholarship, and fellowships from the Guggenheim Foundation, the Bogliasco Foundation, and the National Endowment for the Arts. Her work has appeared in *The New Yorker, The Paris Review, Agni, The Atlantic, Southwest Review, Yale Review, The New Republic, Literary Imagination, Kenyon Review*, and *Best American Poetry* (1989, 1998, and 2009 editions). She teaches at Hofstra University and lives in New York City.

Alexis Levitin's translations have appeared in well over 200 magazines, including *New England Review, APR, Grand Street, Kenyon Review, Mid-American Review*, and *Prairie Schooner*. His thirty-five books include Clarice Lispector's *Soulstorm* and Eugenio de Andrade's *Forbidden Words*, both from New Directions. His most recent books are the Vizcainos collection *Destruction in the Afternoon* from Dialogos Books, a bilingual edition of Salgado Maranhao's *Blood of the Sun* (Milkweed Editions, 2012), a bilingual edition of *Tobacco Dogs* by Ecuadorian Ana

Minga (The Bitter Oleander Press, 2013), and *The Art of Patience* by Eugenio de Andrade (Red Dragonfly Press, 2013).

A winner of the Albanian National Silver Pen Prize in 2000 and the International Kristal Vilenica Prize in 2009, **Luljeta Lleshanaku** is the author of six books of poetry in Albanian. She is also the author of six poetry collections in other languages: *Antipastoral*, 2006, Italy; *Kinder der natur*, 2010, Austria; *Dzieci natury*, 2011, Poland. *Haywire: New & Selected Poems* (Bloodaxe Books, 2011), a finalist for the 2013 Popescu Prize (formerly the European Poetry Translation Prize) by Poetry Society, UK, is her first British publication, and includes work from two editions published in the US by New Directions, *Fresco: Selected Poems* (2002), which drew on four collections published in Albania from 1992 to 1999, and *Child of Nature* (2010), a book of translations of later poems which was a finalist for the 2011 BTBA (Best Translated Book Award). Lleshanaku was also nominated for the European poetry prize The European Poet of Freedom, 2012, in Poland.

William Logan is the author of ten volumes of poetry, most recently *Madame X* (2012). He has published six books of essays and reviews, including *The Undiscovered Country*, which received the National Book Critics Circle award in criticism. A new book of criticism, *Guilty Knowledge, Guilty Pleasure*, was published last year.

Thomas Lux was born in Massachusetts in December 1946 and graduated from Emerson College. He has been awarded grants and fellowships from the Guggenheim Foundation and the Mellon Foundation. He is a three time recipient of NEA grants. In 1994, he was awarded the Kinglsey Tufts Prize for his book, *Split Horizon*. The most recent of his 12 full-length poetry collections is *Child Made of Sand* (Houghton Mifflin Harcourt, 2012). He also recently published *From the Southland* (Marick Press, 2012, nonfiction). BloodAxe Books published *Selected Poems* in the UK in 2014. A book of poems, *Zehntausend Herrliche Jahre*, in German, trs. Klaus Martens, was published in 2011. Currently, he is Bourne Professor of Poetry and Director of the McEver Visiting Writers program at the Georgia Institute of Technology, as well as Director of Poetry @ Tech.

Maurice Manning's most recent books are *The Gone and the Going Away* and *The Rag-Picker's Guide to Poetry*, co-edited with Eleanor Wilner. Manning teaches at Transylvania University and in the MFA Program for Writers at Warren Wilson College. He lives in Kentucky.

Gail Mazur's most recent book is *Figures in a Landscape* (University of Chicago Press, 2011). Forbidden City is forthcoming from U of Chicago Press in 2016. She is author of four earlier books of poetry, *Nightfire, The Pose of Happiness, The Common, They Can't Take That Away from Me* (University of Chicago Press, 2001), which was a finalist for the National Book Award in 2001, and *Zeppo's First Wife: New & Selected Poems*, (Chicago, 2006) won the 2006 Massachusetts Book Award, and was a finalist for the 2005 Los Angeles Times Book Prize and for the 2006 Paterson Poetry Prize. She is Distinguished Writer in Residence in Emerson College's MFA program

Campbell McGrath is the author of many books of poetry, most recently the chapbook *Picasso/Mao* (Upper Rubber Boot, 2014) and the forthcoming *XX: for the 20th Century* (Ecco Press, 2015). He lives in Miami Beach and teaches in the MFA program at Florida International University.

Maureen N. McLane is the author of three books of poems, most recently *This Blue* (FSG, 2014), a Finalist for the National Book Award in Poetry.

Erika Meitner is the author of four books of poems, including *Copia* (BOA Editions, 2014) and *Ideal Cities* (HarperCollins, 2010), which was a 2009 National Poetry Series winner. Her poems have been published in *Best American Poetry, Ploughshares, The New Republic, Virginia Quarterly Review, APR, Tin House,* and elsewhere. She is currently the 2014–15 Fulbright Distinguished Scholar in Creative

Writing at Queen's University, Belfast. She is also an associate professor of English at Virginia Tech, where she teaches in the MFA program.

Drew Milne's recent books of poetry include: *equipollence* (2012), *the view from Royston cave* (2012), *Burnt Laconics Bloom* (2013), and, with John Kinsella, *Reactor Red Shoes* (2013). Previous books include *Sheet Mettle* (1994), *Bench Marks* (1998), *The Damage: new and selected poems* (2001), *Mars Disarmed* (2002), and *Go Figure* (2003). His work is also featured in collections and anthologies, notably *Conductors of Chaos*, edited by Iain Sinclair (1996) and *Anthology of Twentieth-Century British and Irish Poetry*, edited by Keith Tuma (2001). He edits the occasional journal *Parataxis: modernism and modern writing* and the poetry imprint Parataxis Editions. He is a Fellow of Corpus Christi College, Cambridge and, since 1997, he has been the Judith E Wilson Lecturer in Drama & Poetry in the Faculty of English, University of Cambridge.

Nancy Mitchell, a Pushcart Prize 2012 recipient, is the author of two volumes of poetry, *The Near Surround* (Four Way Books, 2002) and *Grief Hut*, (Cervena Barva Press, 2009) and her poems have appeared in *Agni, Poetry Daily, Salt Hill Journal*, and are anthologized in *Last Call* by Sarabande Books. *Make it Sound True*, a teaching exercise using sound as a poetic device is included in *The Working Poet* (Autumn House Press, 2009). She teaches at Salisbury University in Maryland.

Carol Moldaw's most recent book is *So Late, So Soon: New and Selected Poems* (Etruscan Press, 2010). She is the author of four other books of poetry, including *The Lightning Field* (2003), which won the 2002 *FIELD* Poetry Prize; and a novel, *The Widening* (2008). She lives in Santa Fe, NM. carolmoldaw.com

Glenn Mott is author of the book *Analects on a Chinese Screen*, and is currently working with Yunte Huang on an anthology of modern Chinese literature for W. W. Norton. He lives in New York City.

Hoa Nguyen is the author of four full-length collections of poetry including *As Long As Trees Last*, (Wave, 2012) and *Red Juice, Poems 1998–2008* (Wave, 2014). She currently lives in Toronto, Ontario, where she curates a reading series and teaches poetics privately and at Ryerson University. The poem "Napalm Notes" is drawn from *A Thousand Times You Lose Your Treasures*, a work in progress.

D. Nurkse is the author of ten collections of poetry, most recently *A Night in Brooklyn*.

William Olsen's most recent collection of poetry is *Sand Theory* (Northwestern). He teaches in the MFA and Ph.D. creative writing programs at Western Michigan University, where he edits *New Issues Poetry and Prose*. He lives in Kalamazoo.

Dzvinia Orlowsky is a poet and translator. She is the author of five collections of poetry published by Carnegie Mellon University Press, including *A Handful of Bees*, reprinted in 2009 as a Carnegie Mellon Classic Contemporary; *Convertible Night, Flurry of Stones*, recipient of a 2010 Sheila Motton Book Award; and her most recent, *Silvertone*, for which she was named Ohio Poetry Day Association's 2014 Co-Poet of the Year. Her translation from Ukrainian of Alexander Dovzhenko's novella *The Enchanted Desna*, was published by House Between Water in 2006; and Jeff Friedman's and her co-translation of *Memorials,* by Polish Poet Mieczyslaw Jastrun, was published by Dialogos in 2014. She is a Founding Editor of Four Way Books and a recipient of a Pushcart Prize and a Massachusetts Cultural Council poetry grant.

Kathleen Ossip is the author of *The Do-Over, The Cold War*, which was one of *Publishers Weekly*'s best books of 2011; *The Search Engine*, selected by Derek Walcott for the *American Poetry Review*/Honickman First Book Prize; and *Cinephrastics*, a chapbook of movie poems. Her poems have appeared in *Best American Poetry, Best American Magazine Writing*, the *Washington Post, The Paris Review, Poetry, The Believer, A Public Space*, and *Poetry Review* (London). She teaches at The New

School in New York, and she is the co-editor of the poetry review website *SCOUT*.

Alicia Ostriker is a poet and critic. Her thirteenth poetry collection, *The Book of Seventy*, received the 2009 National Jewish Book Award for Poetry; *The Book of Life: Selected Jewish Poems 1979–2011* received a Paterson Lifetime Achievement Award in 2013. She has also received awards from the Poetry Society of America, the San Francisco Poetry Center, the Guggenheim foundation and the Rockefeller Foundation among others, and has twice been a National Book Award finalist. Her most recent book of poems is *The Old Woman, the Tulip, and the Dog*. As a critic, Ostriker is the author of *Stealing the Language: the Emergence of Women's Poetry in America*, and has published several other books on poetry and on the Bible. She is Professor Emerita of Rutgers University, lives in Princeton, NJ and NYC, and teaches in the Low-Residency MFA Program of Drew University.

Linda Pastan's book *Insomnia* will be published by W. W. Norton in fall 2015.

Molly Peacock's newest book is *Alphabetique: 26 Characteristic Fictions*, illustrations by Kara Kosaka (McClelland & Stewart, 2014). Her latest poetry is *The Second Blush* and her recent nonfiction is *The Paper Garden: Mrs. Delany Begins Her Life's Work at 72*. A former New Yorker and instigator of Poetry in Motion, she now lives in Toronto where she serves as Series Editor of *The Best Canadian Poetry*. She writes in dual genres, and she is a dual citizen.

Robert Pinsky's most recent books are his *Selected Poems* and *Singing School*. FSG has re-released the audio version of his *Inferno* of Dante, read by Frank Bidart, Louise Glück, Seamus Heaney and Robert Pinsky.

Lia Purpura is the author of three collections of poems (*King Baby, Stone Sky Lifting*, and *The Brighter the Veil*), three collections of essays (*Rough Likeness, On Looking, Increase*), and one collection of translations, (*Poems of Grzegorz Musial: Berliner Tagebuch and Taste of Ash*). In addition to a 2012 Guggenheim Fellowship, Lia Purpura has also been awarded an NEA Fellowship, a Fulbright Fellowship (Translation, Warsaw, Poland), three Pushcart Prizes, a grant from the Maryland State Arts Council, and multiple residencies and fellowships at the MacDowell Colony. Purpura's poems and essays appear in *Agni, Ecotone, Field, The Georgia Review, Orion, The New Republic, The New Yorker, The Paris Review, Parnassus: Poetry in Review, Ploughshares, The Southern Review* and many other magazines and anthologies, including *Best American Essays 2011* and the *Pushcart Prize Anthology* 30, 34 & 35.

Lawrence Raab is the author of seven collections of poems, most recently *The History of Forgetting* (Penguin, 2009) and *A Cup of Water Turns into a Rose*, a long poem published as a chapbook by Adastra Press (2012). He teaches literature and writing at Williams College.

Barbara Ras is the author of three poetry collections: *Bite Every Sorrow*, which won the Walt Whitman Award and was also awarded the Kate Tufts Discovery Award; *One Hidden Stuff*; and *The Last Skin*, winner of the Award for Poetry from the Texas Institute of Letters. Ras has received fellowships from the John Simon Guggenheim Memorial Foundation and the Rockefeller Foundation, among others. Her poems have appeared in *The New Yorker, Tin House, Granta, American Scholar, Massachusetts Review*, and *Orion*, as well as in many other magazines and anthologies. She is the editor of a collection of short fiction in translation, *Costa Rica: A Traveler's Literary Companion*. Ras lives in San Antonio, where she directs Trinity University Press.

Alberto Ríos is the author of several collections of poetry, including *Dangerous Shirt* (Copper Canyon Press, 2009); *The Smallest Muscle in the Human Body*, which was nominated for the National Book Award; and *Whispering to Fool the Wind*, which won the 1981 Walt Whitman Award.

David Rivard's new collection of poems, *Standoff*, will be published by Graywolf in early 2016. His other books include *Otherwise Elsewhere, Sugartown*, and *Wise Poison*, winner of the James Laughlin Prize from the Academy of American Poets and a finalist for the Los Angeles Times Book Award. He teaches in the MFA in Writing program at the University of New Hampshire.

Clare Rossini has published three collections, the most recent of which is *Lingo*. Work has appeared in *Ploughshares, The Kenyon Review, The Paris Review*, and *Best American Poetry* and has been featured on NPR and the BBC. She is Artist-in-Residence in the English Department at Trinity College in Hartford, CT.

Mary Ruefle's latest book is *Trances of the Blast* (Wave Books, 2103). She lives in Vermont.

Ira Sadoff is the author of eight volumes of poetry; most recently, *Palm Reading in Winter* was reissued in the Carnegie Mellon Contemporary Classics Series. In 2012 BOA Editions published *True Faith*. His other recent poetry collections include *Barter* (2003) and *Grazing* (1998). Poems in *Grazing* have been awarded the Leonard Shestack Prize, the Pushcart Prize, and the George Bogin Memorial Prize from the Poetry Society of America. Since *True Faith*, he has had work in *APR* and *Kenyon Review* and several anthologies. He lives in a converted barn in upstate NY.

Grace Schulman's seventh book of poems is *Without a Claim* (Mariner, Houghton Mifflin Harcourt). Her recent collection of essays is *First Loves and Other Adventures* (U of Michigan Press, 2010). Among her honors are the Aiken Taylor Award for poetry, the Delmore Schwartz Memorial Award, a Guggenheim Fellowship, and five Pushcart prizes. Editor of *The Poems of Marianne Moore* (Viking, 2003), she is Distinguished Professor of English at Baruch College, CUNY. She is a former director of the Poetry Center, 92nd Street Y, 1974–84, and former poetry editor of *The Nation*, 1971–2006.

Martha Serpas has published three collections of poetry, *Côte Blanche, The Dirty Side of the Storm*, and *The Diener*. Her work has appeared in *The New Yorker, The New York Times, The Nation*, and *Southwest Review*. She is on the faculty of the Creative Writing Program at the University of Houston and also serves as a hospital trauma chaplain.

Born and raised in Boston, MA, **Alan Shapiro** is the author of 12 books of poetry, including *Night of the Republic*, a finalist for both the National Book Award and The Griffin Prize; two memoirs, (; *The Last Happy Occasion*, which was a finalist for the National Book Circle Critics Award in autobiography, and *Vigil*; a novel, *Broadway Baby*; a book of critical essays, *In Praise of the Impure: Poetry and the Ethical Imagination*; and two translations, *The Oresteia* by Aeschylus and *The Trojan Women* by Euripides, both published by Oxford University Press. He has won numerous awards, including The Kingsley Tufts Award, LA Times Book Prize, The O.B. Hardison Award from the Folger Shakespeare Library, The William Carlos Williams Award from the Poetry Society of America, an award in literature from The American Academy of Arts and Letters, two NEAs, a Guggenheim and a Lila Wallace Reader's Digest Award. He is also a member of the American Academy of Arts and Sciences. His new book of poems, *Reel to Reel*, was published in April 2014, from University of Chicago Press. He has taught at Stanford University, Northwestern University, Warren Wilson College (in its low-residency MFA program for writers), and since 1995 has been on the faculty at the University of North Carolina where he is the William R. Kenan, Jr. Distinguished Professor of English and Creative Writing.

Eleni Sikelianos is the author of, most recently *The Loving Detail of the Living & the Dead* (Coffee House Press, 2013), *Body Clock* (2008), *The Book of Jon* (City Lights Publishers, 2004), *The California Poem* (Coffee House Press, 2004), *The Monster Lives of Boys & Girls* (Green Integer, 2003), *Earliest Worlds* (Coffee House Press, 2001), *The Book of Tendons* (Post-Apollo Press, 1997), and *To Speak While Dreaming* (Selva Editions, 1993). She teaches in and directs the Creative Writing program at the University of Denver, and is guest faculty for the Naropa Summer Writing Program.

Jeffrey Skinner's latest collection of poems is *Glaciology*. His more recent work has appeared or is forthcoming in *Verse, Slate*, and the *Kenyon* and *Yale Reviews*, among other journals. He is the recipient of a 2014 Guggenheim Fellowship in poetry.

Floyd Skloot's most recent book is *Revertigo: An Off-Kilter Memoir* (University of Wisconsin Press, 2014). His eighth collection of poems, *Approaching Winter*, will be published by Louisiana State University Press in fall 2015.

John Skoyles is the author of four books of poems and three of prose, most recently *A Moveable Famine: A Life in Poetry*. He teaches at Emerson College and is the poetry editor of *Ploughshares*.

Ron Slate has published two books of poems, *The Incentive of the Maggot* (2005) and *The Great Wave* (2008), both via Houghton Mifflin Harcourt. He writes about books at "On the Seawall" (ronslate.com) and recently became a board member of Mass Humanities.

Bruce Smith is the author of six books of poems, most recently *Devotions*, a finalist for the National Book Award, the National Book Critics Circle Awards, the LA Times Book Award, and the winner of the William Carlos Williams Prize.

Charlie Smith has written eight poetry books, including *Jump Soul: New and Selected Poems* (W. W. Norton, 2014), eight novels, including *Ginny Gall*, forthcoming from Harper Perennial, 2016, and a book of novellas. Five NY Times Notable Books. Aga Khan Prize. Levinson Prize.

Ron Smith is the author of the books *Its Ghostly Workshop* (2013), *Moon Road: Poems 1986–2005* (2007), and *Running Again in Hollywood Cemetery* (1988). In July, he was named Poet Laureate of Virginia.

Lisa Russ Spaar is the author and editor of ten books, most recently *Vanitas, Rough: Poems* (Persea, 2012) and *The Hide-and-Seek Muse: Annotations of Contemporary Poetry* (Drunken Boat, 2013). Her awards include a Rona Jaffe Award, a Guggenheim Fellowship, the Library of Virginia Prize, and the Carole Weinstein Award for Poetry. Her essays and reviews appear in *The New York Times*, the *Chronicle of Higher Education*, the *Los Angeles Review of Books*, and elsewhere. She is Professor of English and Creative Writing at the University of Virginia.

Jane Springer is author of *Dear Blackbird* and *Murder Ballad*. Her honors include a Pushcart, an NEA fellowship, a *Best American Poetry* prize, and a Whiting Writers' Award. She lives in upstate New York with her husband, their son and their two dogs, Leisure-Lee and Azy.

Page Hill Starzinger lives in New York City. Her first full-length poetry book, *Vestigial* (2013), was selected by Lynn Emanuel to win the Barrow Street Book Prize. Her poems have appeared in *Kenyon Review, Colorado Review, Fence, Pleiades, Volt*, and many others.

Terese Svoboda's *When the Next Big War Blows Down the Valley: Selected and New Poems* is forthcoming from Anhinga Press, 2015. *Anything That Burns You: Lola Ridge, Radical Poet* will be published by Schaffner Press in 2016.

Brian Swann's most recent publications are *In Late Light* (Johns Hopkins University Press, 2013) (poetry) and *Sky Loom: Native American Myth, Story, and Song* (University of Nebraska Press, 2014).

Cole Swensen is the author of fourteen collections of poetry, most recently *Gravesend*. She teaches at Brown University and runs a nano-press dedicated to contemporary French poetry in translation, La Presse (lapressepoetry.com).

Arthur Sze published three books in 2014: his ninth book of poetry, *Compass Rose* (Copper Canyon), a collaboration with artist Susan York,

The Unfolding Center (Radius Books), and a Chinese/English selected poems, *Pig's Heaven Inn* (Beijing: Intellectual Property Publishing House). He received the 2013 Jackson Poetry Prize and is a chancellor of the Academy of American Poets.

In 2013, **John Taylor** won the Raiziss-de Palchi Translation Fellowship from the Academy of American Poets for his project to translate the poetry of Lorenzo Calogero. This project will be published by Chelsea Editions. Otherwise, Taylor has recently translated books by Philippe Jaccottet, Jacques Dupin, José-Flore Tappy, Louis Calaferte, and Pierre-Albert Jourdan. His most recent personal book is *If Night is Falling* (Bitter Oleander Press).

Daniel Tobin is the author of five previous books of poems, *Where the World is Made, Double Life, The Narrows, Second Things*, and *Belated Heavens* (winner of the Massachusetts Book Award in Poetry, 2011), along with the critical studies *Passage to the Center* and *Awake in America*. He is the editor of *The Book of Irish American Poetry from the Eighteenth Century to the Present, Light in Hand: The Selected Early Poems* and *Lola Ridge*, and (with Pimone Triplett) *Poet's Work, Poet's Play: Essays on the Practice and the Art*. His awards include the "Discovery" / The Nation Award, the Robert Penn Warren Award, the Robert Frost Fellowship, the Katharine Bakeless Nason Prize, and creative writing fellowships from the National Endowment for the Arts and the John Simon Guggenheim Foundation.

Georg Trakl (1887–1914). Austrian expressionist poet Trakl's work, influenced by French impressionist poetry, reveals his disgust with imperialistic society. An absorption with sorrow and decay permeates his *Gedichte* [Poems] (1913), the only collection published during his lifetime. A pharmacist in the German army, Trakl died from a drug overdose. Posthumous publications of his work include *Der Herbst des Einsamen* [The Autumn of the Lonely] (1920) and *Gesang des Abgeschiedenen* [Song of the Departed] (1933).

William Trowbridge's latest collection is *Put This On, Please: New and Selected Poems* (Red Hen Press, 2014). His other collections are *Ship of Fool, The Complete Book of Kong, Flickers, O Paradise*, and *Enter Dark Stranger*. He teaches in the University of Nebraska Low-residency MFA in Writing Program and is currently Poet Laureate of Missouri. williamtrowbridge.net.

Chase Twichell's most recent book is *Horses Where the Answers Should Have Been: New & Selected Poems* (Copper Canyon, 2010), which won both the Kingsley Tufts Award from Claremont Graduate University and the Balcones Poetry Prize. She splits the year between the Adirondacks and Miami.

Marc Vincenz is British-Swiss and has published eight collections of poetry; his latest are *This Wasted Land and its Chymical Illuminations* (Lavender Ink) and *Becoming the Sound of Bees* (Ampersand Books). He is the translator of several German-language poets, including the Herman Hesse Prize winner, Klaus Merz. His most recent book of translations is Erika Burkart's *A Late Recognition of the Signs* (Spuyten Duyvil, 2014). His own work has been translated into German, Russian, Romanian, French and Chinese. He has been awarded numerous grants from the Swiss Arts council and a fellowship from the Literarisches Colloquium, Berlin. He has lived in England, Switzerland, Hong Kong and China, but recently moved to the United States and now resides in Cambridge, MA.

Santiago Vizcaíno's first book of poetry, *Destruction in the Afternoon*, won the Premio Proyectos Literarios Nacionales award from the Ecuadorian Ministry of Culture in 2008, published in English by Bill Lavender/Dialogos Books. His second book, *In the Twilight*, won second prize in the Pichincha Poetry Prize competition in 2010. His work has appeared in *Bitter Oleander, Connotation Press, Dirty Goat, Eleven/Eleven, eXchanges, Ezra, Lake Effect, Osiris, Per Contra, Rowboat, Saranac Review*, and *Words Without Borders*.

Arthur Vogelsang's books of poetry are *A Planet* (Holt, 1983), *Twentieth Century Women* (University of Georgia Press, 1988), which was selected by John Ashbery for the Contemporary Poetry Series, *Cities and Towns* (University of Massachusetts Press, 1996), which received the Juniper Prize, *Left Wing of a Bird* (Sarabande, 2003), and *Expedition: New & Selected Poems* (Ashland Poetry Press, 2011), with numerous appearances in anthologies such as *Best American Poetry* (Scribner), the *Pushcart Prize Anthology, The New Breadloaf Anthology of Contemporary Poetry*, and *American Hybrid* (W.W. Norton). He was an editor/publisher of *The American Poetry Review* 1973–2006. He has poems in recent or forthcoming issues of *Boston Review, Gettysburg Review, The North American Review, The New Yorker, Poetry, Poetry Daily*, and *The Yale Review*.

Karen Volkman is the author of *Nomina* (BOA Editions, 2008); *Spar* (University of Iowa Press, 2002), winner of the James Laughlin Award and the Iowa Poetry Prize; and *Crash's Law*, which was selected for the National Poetry Series by Heather McHugh.

Diane Wakoski has published 21 books of poetry, and her work has appeared at numerous periodicals, including *CounterPunch*. Her most recent book is *Bay of Angels* (2013, Anhinga Press). A pillar of the "Beat Movement," her life and work have inspired generations of American and international writers.

G. C. Waldrep's most recent books are *The Arcadia Project: North American Postmodern Pastoral* (Ahsahta, 2012), co-edited with Joshua Corey, and a chapbook, *Susquehanna* (Omnidawn, 2013). BOA Editions will release a long poem, *Testament*, in May 2015. Waldrep lives in Lewisburg, Pa., where he teaches at Bucknell University, edits the journal *West Branch*, and serves as Editor-at-Large for *The Kenyon Review*.

Rosanna Warren teaches in the Committee on Social Thought at the University of Chicago. Her most recent book of poems is *Ghost in a Red Hat* (W. W. Norton, 2012).

Afaa Michael Weaver (aka Michael S. Weaver) is a native of Baltimore. A poet, playwright, and translator, he is the author of fourteen collections of poetry and several plays. A graduate of Brown University's creative writing program (1985–87), his awards include National Endowment for the Arts and Pew fellowships, as well as three Pushcart prizes. In playwriting he has received the PDI award. Recent poetry collections include *A Hard Summation* (Central Square Press) and the book that concludes his Plum Flower Trilogy, *City of Eternal Spring* (Pitt Poetry Series); his new play is *GRIP*. Weaver holds an endowed chair at Simmons College and teaches in Drew University's low-residency MFA program. In 2014 he received the Kingsley Tufts Award for *The Government of Nature* (U of Pittsburgh Press). His poetry is included in 2014 & 2015 *Best American Poetry*. afaaweaver. net and plumflowertrilogy.org

Charles Harper Webb has published eight books of poetry, including *Reading the Water, Liver, Tulip Farms & Leper Colonies, Hot Popsicles*, and *Amplified Dog*. *Shadow Ball: New and Selected Poems* was published in 2009 by University of Pittsburgh Press. His latest book, *Brain Camp*, was published by the University of Pittsburgh Press in 2015. His awards in poetry include the Morse Prize, the Kate Tufts Discovery Award, the Felix Pollock Prize, and the Benjamin Saltman Prize. His poems have appeared in *American Poetry Review, The Paris Review, Iowa Review, Ploughshares, Michigan Quarterly Review, Poets of the New Century, Best American Poetry*, and the *Pushcart Prize Anthology*.

Dara Wier is the author of numerous collections of poetry, most recently *You Good Thing* (Wave Books, 2013). Her work has appeared in *American Poetry Review, Boston Review, jubilat*, and *New American Writing*, among other magazines.

Scott Withiam's first book, *Arson & Prophets*, is published by Ashland Poetry Press. His poems are recently out in *Agni, Antioch Review, Ascent, Boston Review, Chattahoochee Review, Cimarron Review,*

Diagram, and *Salamander.* Poems are forthcoming in *Barrow Street* and *Beloit Poetry Journal.* He works for a non-profit in the Boston area.

C. D. Wright has published over a dozen titles of poetry and prose. Her most recent book, *One With Others,* a little book of her days, won the Lenore Marshall Prize and the National Book Critics Circle Award. In 2015 she will publish a prose work, *The Poet, The Lion, Talking Picutres, El Farolito, A Wedding at St. Roch, The Big Box Store, The Warp in the Mirror, Spring, Midnights, Fire and All,* followed by a collection of poems, *ShallCross.*

Monica Youn's third book of poems, *Blackacre,* is forthcoming from Graywolf Press in 2016. Her second book, *Ignatz* (Four Way Books, 2010), was a finalist for the National Book Award, and her poems have been widely published in magazines and anthologies, including *The New Yorker, Poetry,* and *Best American Poetry.* She has been awarded fellowships from the Library of Congress, the Rockefeller Foundation, and Stanford University, among other awards. A former lawyer, she now teaches poetry at Princeton University and at the Warren Wilson College MFA for Writers.

夏宇 **Hsia Yü** is one of the most innovative and influential poets in the Chinese-speaking world and a noted song lyricist and award-winning book designer. The poem translated here is from her most recent collection, *Poems, Sixty of Them.* She lives in Taipei.

CPSIA information can be obtained at www.ICGtesting.com
Printed in the USA
BVOW05s1133220815

414533BV00001B/2/P